CHAMPION'S CHALLENGE!

Holiday club programme
for 5- to 11-year-olds

© Helen Franklin 2007
First published 2007
ISBN 978 1 84427 270 9

Scripture Union, 207–209 Queensway, Bletchley, Milton Keynes, MK2 2EB, UK
Email: info@scriptureunion.org.uk
Website: www.scriptureunion.org.uk

Scripture Union Australia, Locked Bag 2, Central Coast Business Centre, NSW 2252, Australia
Website: www.scriptureunion.org.au

Scripture Union USA, PO Box 987, Valley Forge, PA 19482, USA
Website: www.scriptureunion.org

Bible quotations have been taken from the Contemporary English Version © American Bible Society. Anglicisations © British and Foreign Bible Society 1996. Published by HarperCollinsPublishers and used with permission.

British Library Cataloguing-in-Publication Data
A catalogue for this book is available from the British Library.

Cover design by Kevin Wade, kwgraphicdesign
Cover and internal illustration by Adrian Barclay
Printed and bound in Great Britain by Henry Ling, Dorchester

The CHAMPION'S CHALLENGE website – www.scriptureunion.org.uk/championschallenge

Visit the CHAMPION'S CHALLENGE website to access downloadable versions of the photocopiable resources and the memory verse song, to read about other people's experiences and check the advice given by other users on the bulletin board.

CHAMPION'S CHALLENGE is part of eye level, Scripture Union's project to catch up with children and young people who have not yet caught sight of Jesus.

Scripture Union is an international Christian charity working with churches in more than 130 countries, providing resources to bring the good news of Jesus Christ to children, young people and families and to encourage them to develop spiritually through the Bible and prayer.

As well as our network of volunteers, staff and associates who run holidays, church-based events and school Christian groups, we produce a wide range of publications and support those who use our resources through training programmes.

For Sarah Mayers, a great editor and brilliant friend, who loved to help children and young people get to know God.

With thanks to St John's Church, Kenilworth for running a trial of Champion's Challenge and all the others who helped out.

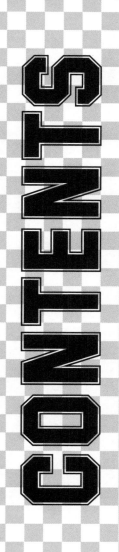

CONTENTS

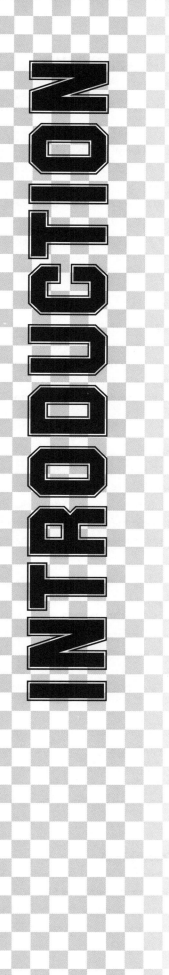

INTRODUCTION

CHAMPION'S CHALLENGE is a five-day children's holiday club programme that focuses on events from Jesus' life, death and resurrection, and on sport. It is based on Luke's Gospel and is packed with creative teaching, games, songs, prayers, craft, Bible reading and small-group ideas, along with a drama script for each day. CHAMPION'S CHALLENGE provides a mixture of small-group activities and up-front presentations. The material includes two family services – one designed to launch the holiday club and the other to round it off. Alternatively, these could be used to extend the programme to seven days.

Additional resources are:

CHAMPION'S CHALLENGE DVD

This includes five storytelling episodes straight from the studio of First-Century Sportscene! The DVD also contains the CHAMPION'S CHALLENGE song, the *Learn and remember* verse song, backing tracks, training material on extending your club beyond the summer and additional resources.

MATCHDAY PROGRAMME

This is a 48-page booklet containing the key passages from Luke's Gospel, along with extra information, puzzles and material to use in small-group meetings. This is ideal for use with 8 to 11s. *Team Sheets* for under-8s are available in this resource (as well as on the DVD-ROM section of the DVD and on the website). These can be used in the small-group sessions or be taken home. Both the *Matchday Programme* and *Team Sheets* will help maintain contact with children's homes and act as a reminder, in the weeks after the club, of what the children experienced at CHAMPION'S CHALLENGE.

More information on these and other resources can be found on the inside front cover. For details of all the resources produced by CPO, see the inside back cover. (CPO resources are not available through Scripture Union.)

CHAMPION'S CHALLENGE TERMINOLOGY

Presenters
The two main up-front presenters of CHAMPION'S CHALLENGE.

Ground Staff
The team of leaders and other volunteers who keep CHAMPION'S CHALLENGE running.

Teams
The small groups that the children will be part of. Activities in teams include refreshments, Bible reading, listening and prayer, games and craft. The teams are led by team captains.

Team dugout
The area where each team meets.

Team time
The time at the start and end of the club, where children spend time in their teams.

Grandstand
The 'all-together' element of CHAMPION'S CHALLENGE. This includes singing, teaching, the drama and more.

Change ends
Small-group Bible exploration, games and craft.

1
THE PROGRAMME

THE AIMS OF CHAMPION'S CHALLENGE

CHAMPION'S CHALLENGE takes children through Luke's Gospel to discover more about Jesus. It will:

- Give them a fun and active week.
- Offer them the opportunity to discover God's love for them shown in Jesus, his Son.
- Explain who Jesus is; what he did as he lived on earth as a man and why his death and resurrection are so important.
- Allow them to hear what it means to follow Jesus today, as they talk with adult Christians.

HOW IT'S DONE

CHAMPION'S CHALLENGE uses the tried-and-tested mix of small-group 'Team time' activities as well as 'Grandstand' presentations. It contains creative Bible teaching, ideas for games and craft, questions to start discussions, a drama script and scoring systems for a daily quiz.

THEME AND SETTING

CHAMPION'S CHALLENGE has a sporty theme. Transform your venue with sports items such as posters, equipment, supporters' scarves and shirts that cover a range of sports; avoid focusing on just one or two if possible, which might exclude some children.

Each day's title uses a different sporting image to explain a different facet of who Jesus is. Key elements in the 'Grandstand' part of the programme are: telling the Bible story, either with the CHAMPION'S CHALLENGE DVD or using the alternative storytelling methods given in each day's programme; suggestions for testimonies that relate the themes to what it means to follow Jesus today; plus a drama that sets the issues firmly in the world of a child.

Key elements in 'Team time' are: Bible exploration in small groups, either using *Matchday Programme* (the separate book for 8 to 11s), or the *Team Sheets* in this resource book for 5 to 8s; time to get to know each other and time to discuss reactions to the Bible teaching.

THE TEACHING PROGRAMME

Ask adults who Jesus is and they might use titles such as 'Son of God', 'Good Shepherd', 'Friend of Sinners' but ask children who have no experience of church and they may well look at you blankly and say 'I don't know!' or even 'Who is Jesus?'

CHAMPION'S CHALLENGE aims to help these children, as well as those who are familiar with Christian teaching, to discover more about Jesus through the roles of people involved with sports teams. So here you will find the selector and trainer, physio and teammate, substitute, winner and, of course, champion. Through these the children will discover how Jesus chose, taught and worked alongside his team, had the power to heal sick people, took the place of someone else when the punishment was being meted out, but yet won the battle against death and destruction so that he is the champion for ever!

This Bible teaching is the most important part of the programme, whether it comes through discussion in 'Team times', storytelling in 'Grandstand' or the application of it in real life that is explained through the interview. This should all be well prayed through, prepared and presented to allow God's Word to settle in children's minds, so that the Holy Spirit has the material to work on for the rest of their lives.

Alongside this is the importance of how you relate to the children, as this gives the Bible teaching credibility. Jesus said, 'When you welcome even a child because of me, you welcome me. And when you welcome me, you welcome the one who sent me' (Luke 9:48). So as you welcome them you are welcoming Jesus; as you talk with them, listen to their stories, laugh at their jokes and cheer their successes. However ordinary they may be, you are doing these things as if to Jesus. Treat them with the love, respect and dignity with which you would honour him.

CHAMPION'S CHALLENGE covers five days, together with two Sunday services. If you are running a club which is shorter than five days, then do Days 4 and 5 together with your choice of Days 1 to 3. Choose which ones best fit the aims of your club.

Sunday 1: SELECTOR
Premier passage: Luke 6:12–16

Premier theme: Jesus chooses his disciples. All are there for a reason.

Premier aims: To launch CHAMPION'S CHALLENGE; to introduce Jesus as God's Son who chose a team to work with him. If this is your regular Sunday service, to help the whole church to have an understanding of what is happening this week.

Day 1: TRAINER
Premier passage: Luke 6:46–49

Premier theme: Jesus teaches his followers about hearing and obeying.

Premier aims: To help the children settle into the club; to teach the importance of the Bible and the wisdom of hearing and obeying what Jesus says.

Day 2: PHYSIO
Premier passage: Luke 7:1–10

Premier theme: Jesus heals people. He has power over illness – even at a distance.

Premier aims: To help the children grasp who Jesus is, and that as God's Son, everything made by God – even sick bodies – has to obey him. To explain the meaning of faith.

Day 3: TEAMMATE
Premier passage: Luke 9:1–6,10–17

Premier theme: Working with Jesus. Everyone has a part to play.

Premier aims: To show that Jesus had lots of people on his team and each one had a part to play. It is the same today: everyone who follows Jesus has a special job to do for him.

Day 4: SUBSTITUTE
Premier passage: Luke 22:47–53; 23

Premier theme: Jesus takes the punishment in our place.

Premier aims: To understand that Jesus had done nothing wrong but was killed because the leaders were jealous of him. They didn't like him telling them they weren't doing things God's way. God used this to do something amazing…

Day 5: WINNER
Premier passage: Luke 24:1–35

Premier theme: Jesus is alive! Jesus defeats death and is alive for ever! He appears to followers and explains the good news.

Premier aims: To ensure the children know that Jesus came alive again, and is alive today!

Sunday 2: CHAMPION
Premier passage: Acts 1:1–8

Premier theme: Jesus promises his Holy Spirit as the disciples' helper.

Premier aims: To show that the Holy Spirit came as Jesus promised, and to explain how he is at work today.

A SAMPLE PROGRAMME

ACTIVITY	RUNNING TIME	INCLUDES
Ground staff	30 minutes	Spiritual and practical preparation
Team time	10 minutes	Introductory activity in teams
Grandstand 1	40 minutes	Songs Jokes Drama Bible Narrative Interview
Change ends	45 minutes	Bible exploration Craft Games
Grandstand 2	20 minutes	Songs Quiz Champion's Challenge Prayer
Team time	5 minutes	A final activity, sometimes prayer, before leaving
Warm down	30 minutes +	Clearing up Debrief Preparation for tomorrow

PROGRAMME BREAKDOWN

Each day's programme contains the following elements:

GROUND STAFF PREPARATION

Aims – be sure everyone knows what you are aiming to achieve through the day's session.

Ground Staff briefing – notes are provided for the spiritual preparation of the Ground Staff. Make time to pray too, and encourage people with what God is doing among children and adults.

Equipment checklist – resources needed for teams and the up-front presenters.

ARRIVING AT CHAMPION'S CHALLENGE

The first moments at CHAMPION'S CHALLENGE are so important! You never get a second chance to make a first impression as they say, so be welcoming, but not overwhelming in putting children and adults at ease. Strike a balance between helping parents to see that their child will be safe with you and giving children a sense of the fun that they will have with you. Make sure that there are sufficient people at the registration desk to show children and their parents to the right teams. It is always helpful to have someone available to answer questions as parents leave, or to remind them of the collection time, or just to say a cheerful 'Goodbye – see you later!'

Registration

Make sure that the registration desk is well organised with spare forms and pens for any parents who want to register children at the door. Have a floor plan of your venue to show where each team is sited so that parents can find their way round. If possible have a large plan available a little distance from the desk so that parents dropping children at more than one team can go back to check the layout without clogging the registration area.

Even if you are keeping central registers at the desk, team captains need a copy of who is in their group each day. They should keep these with them at all times so that in the event of a fire they can quickly check that everyone in their team and be sure is safely out of the building.

Team time 1

This section is not just a fill-in until the last child arrives! It is a great opportunity for Ground Staff and captains to get to know their teams, to recap the previous day or set the scene for each day's activities. Your priorities as Ground Staff are to get to know the children and help them to settle; theirs will be to play the game or complete the activity. Try to get a balance between the two early on, to allow everyone to get the most from this time.

GRANDSTAND 1

This section of the programme should have something of the pace and fun of weekend children's television. Younger children may struggle to keep up with things that are too fast, so give them a chance to think and answer whilst keeping the attention of older ones. Activities are led from the front but teams need to sit around their captains.

Warm-up exercises

Use these to get the children ready for what is ahead. Play some lively music in the background, if possible with a sporting connection. Keep the actions simple but build up the number of different ones through the week. If children have registered in advance check for any special needs and include some actions that will be easy for them; try to include options for children who are sitting as well as more active movements.

Slam Dunk basket

Use a basket as a receptacle for jokes, letters to the presenters or pictures that could be displayed around the walls.

Champion team challenge

This activity is done in teams, each huddled round their captain. It involves minimal equipment and no preparation. Team captains will need to write down the answers some days so should have pen and paper ready.

'Wembley Way' drama

Although there are humorous situations in this drama, the feel is more *Byker Grove* than *The Chuckle Brothers*. It aims to resonate with the children's world and so uses realistic characters, rather than larger-than-life ones. Each episode links to the day's theme.

Songs

Choose a mix of songs that children who come to church regularly will know and others that are new to everyone. If you have children coming who are not used to church, avoid songs that express belief or faith and keep them factual ('God is' or 'Jesus did' rather than 'I believe'). Children will enjoy music from a live band, but use CDs or tapes and good quality sound equipment if a band is not possible, and this will work just as well.

Bible teaching

Use either the CHAMPION'S CHALLENGE DVD or the script given in each day's outline.

Match of the day

Interview one of the Ground Staff about following Jesus. It gives an opportunity for the children to discover how the Bible's teaching relates to everyday life for those who follow Jesus. Not everything that God does in people's lives is appropriate for children so choose testimonies with care.

The bench

This is a designated 'quiet area' within your main working area, where children can go for some space and peace. It is NOT a 'naughty corner' although it may be used as a cooling off place for a child who is struggling with their behaviour. It offers a quiet place for any child who is tired or unable to cope with the programme, but its main use should be as an area where children can talk one-to-one with Ground Staff. It should therefore be in sight of other leaders at all times. The overall leader should keep a check on any children who are in this area and encourage them to rejoin their group as soon as possible unless talking with one of the ground staff.

CHANGE ENDS

This section allows time for children and Ground Staff to build friendships, to discover more about the Bible teaching, to create something that will act as a lasting reminder of it, and to burn off some energy in a sporting way! The ideal would be to have everything set up before the programme begins but with limited space this may not be possible. You may therefore decide to do just two of the three sections each day. If so, be sure to include 'Time out' every day but vary the other sections.

If you have enough space you might choose to run all three activities at the same time in different parts of the premises, moving groups from one activity to the next, which means having fewer children on each activity.

Time out

This is an opportunity for refreshments but also for the children to look at the day's passage in more depth. Remember to provide some healthy snacks as well as biscuits, and check that what you serve is suitable for any children with food allergies. Be creative with what you do: if you have the space, set up a cafe area with tables and chairs. Chat briefly over drinks but do be sure to allow enough time for your Bible exploration (using the *Matchday Programme* or *Team Sheets*). Be aware that younger children will take a surprisingly long time to eat a biscuit and drink some squash! This time allows captains to check if the children have understood the story, and develops the children's skills in thinking about the meaning of the Bible.

Trophy room

Making a craft activity has two particular purposes: it gives the children something to take home from the club that will act as a reminder; also the time spent making it is a good opportunity for Ground Staff to chat with their teams. You may find that you can have deeper conversations in this time – when everyone is busy looking at their craft – than when you have eye contact in 'Time out'. Therefore, make good use of the time to build friendships and chat about the day's teaching a little more, especially in relation to the children's lives. From the Ground Staff's point of view, this conversation should be as important as the craft! See the craft ideas bank for craft with a sport's theme.

Stadium

It would be odd not to include some games in CHAMPION'S CHALLENGE. In the games ideas bank there are team games, general games and ideas for personal best, an opportunity for each child to try a selection of sports and improve at these through the week. This book includes a template for a certificate recognising the improvement (see page 39), which can be given to each child at the end of the week.

GRANDSTAND 2

A question of sport (and other things!)

Most children love quizzes, not least for the rivalry between different teams and the delight of winning. However, they can take a long time to run so keep them fast-moving. Use a mix of questions on general knowledge, sports and the day's Bible passage. Avoid those that demand very specialist knowledge so that anyone can answer. Keep the style of questions varied (such as asking for a straight answer, providing a choice of two or three answers, or even using pictures for some questions).

Champion's Challenge

Through the week the children will learn Luke 9:23, a key verse in this Gospel. They need to know what the verse means as well as knowing the actual words, as 'take up your cross each day' sounds very scary! To this end, explanations are given.

TEAM TIME 2

This is not just filling in time until parents come to collect their children, although it will allow you to keep children occupied until that happens. Some days this is a specific activity, such as prayer, so have all the team sitting down, getting on with the activity from Day 1. Try to avoid making a big issue of people going home so that the focus stays on the activity for children who are last to be collected. Be sure to check children out from the registers as they leave the team dugout!

WARM DOWN

It may be that some of your Ground Staff have their own children at CHAMPION'S CHALLENGE and are unable to stay for long when the programme ends. As a minimum, have everyone together to check any problems, briefly remind people of tomorrow's activities, and pray for God's Word to be at work in the children. Then any further preparation can be done.

If you can find willing volunteers to do this, have a team come in to help with clearing up and preparation. There may even be people who could bring in a snack lunch for the team to eat before they start on this work!

OTHER ELEMENTS OF CHAMPION'S CHALLENGE

Services

Starting CHAMPION'S CHALLENGE with a church service the Sunday before the club is a good way of getting the church praying for the club and commissioning the leaders. A service after the club will round things up nicely and be a good event to invite parents to. Outlines for these services are on pages 46 and 47.

Under-5s resources

For details of resources to use with under-5s in your teams, visit the CHAMPION'S CHALLENGE website at: www.scriptureunion.org.uk/championschallenge

11 to 14s resources

For details of resources to use with 11 to 14s, visit the CHAMPION'S CHALLENGE website at: www.scriptureunion.org.uk/championschallenge

Following up CHAMPION'S CHALLENGE

A holiday club lasts only a short time – what about the rest of the year? How are you going to stay in contact with those children who have no other connection with church apart from the holiday club? Planning follow-up is as vital as planning for the club itself – see page 79. Maybe you could start a midweek club (see inside front cover for details of *Target Challenge*, the follow-up programme to CHAMPION'S CHALLENGE), build up links with your local primary schools and offer to take assemblies or give out copies of *It's Your Move*! to Year 6 children as they move on to secondary school. For ideas and advice, contact Scripture Union on 01908 856170 or your local schools work trust.

2
PLANNING YOUR PROGRAMME

PLANNING CHAMPION'S CHALLENGE

DEFINE YOUR AIMS

The broad aims of CHAMPION'S CHALLENGE are outlined on page 8, but it is important to think about the specific aims that you might have for your club. These will affect the way you set up, promote and run your programme. What kind of children do you want to attract to your club? Will it be a club for all the children in your area? Do you hope to reach out specifically to those children who have had no previous church background (and so present the gospel to those who have never heard it)? Do you wish to nurture the children who are already connected to your church and get to know them better? How many children do you hope to accommodate? One of your aims might be to reach as many children as possible. This will depend on the size of your venue, the number of leaders you have and any financial constraints you have to work under. You may wish to limit the age range – that way you can reach a greater number of a more specific group, maybe an age range of which your church has only a small number. Do you want to use the club as a way of making links between your church fellowship and local families? What are your aims for your team? Do you want to develop the gifts and abilities of the leaders you have available? Is it one of your aims that the club should be a project the church can get behind and work on together? Will the club enable several churches to work together?

CHOOSE YOUR DATES

You'll need to fix the date for your holiday club early enough for people to take it into account when they book their holidays. But you'll also need to take into account other activities that may clash:

- Other holiday clubs in the area
- Other activities already booked at your premises
- Holidays organised by local schools
- Holidays/camps for local Boys' Brigade, Girls' Brigade, Cub or Brownie groups
- Festivals etc taking place in your local area.

There will be similar questions about when your potential leaders are available. In fact, the leaders' availability will have a big impact on the duration of your holiday club. If most of your leaders need to take time off work, it may not be practical to run a full five-day club.

LEGAL REQUIREMENTS

There are various legal requirements you will need to be familiar with and conform to as you prepare for your holiday club. These include: registering your event with OFSTED; having a child protection policy in operation to recruit the team; providing adequate space at the venue; having sufficient adult to child ratios and being covered by insurance. To obtain up-to-date information on all of these requirements go to www.scriptureunion.org. uk/championschallenge

PUBLICITY

The best way to ensure you have plenty of children at your holiday club is for the event to be well publicised. There is material available from CPO to help you with this. See the inside back cover for details. Here are some things to consider:

Posters and flyers

Use these to advertise CHAMPION'S CHALLENGE.

Letters and forms

How about sending a letter or invitation card to every child your church has contact with? Or you might distribute letters to all the children in your area, maybe through the local schools. Your letter could enclose an application/registration form to be returned to you. You may also need a follow-up letter, which will enclose a consent/medical form, and perhaps a CHAMPION'S CHALLENGE badge.

School assemblies

You may have a local Christian schools worker, or people from your church who are involved in schools ministry. Or you may have some church members who are teachers. If so, they could promote your CHAMPION'S CHALLENGE event in a school assembly, if the school is happy for them to do so.

Prayer cards/bookmarks

It is important to keep your church informed about your event. Prayer cards or prayer bookmarks can help your church members pray for your holiday club – before, during and after your CHAMPION'S CHALLENGE event.

PLAN IN DETAIL

In the few months before CHAMPION'S CHALLENGE, you'll need to consider and organise the following aspects.

Presentation and teaching

How will you adapt the material to suit your particular age group(s)? What audio/visual aids will you need? Will you need amplification or video projection equipment? Who will be the presenters?

Programme priorities

You may not have time to fit in all the activities that are suggested. Within team times – especially during 'Time out' – you could get so engrossed in general conversation that you never start on the Bible discussions, so be sure to plan carefully.

Imagine filling a jar up to the top with pebbles. You might think it is now full, but try adding some smaller stones and you'll find there is room for them. Is it full now? Try pouring in water, and you will see that only then is the jar really full. But if you put in this amount of either small stones or water first you would not then get everything in! When planning, make sure you put in the essentials first – Bible teaching through the DVD or drama, and discussion time in groups. Then add the less vital but still important things, and finally the parts that 'fill it up'.

Music

Choose the songs for the week, and gather the musicians together to rehearse them. It's good to have a number of musicians playing a variety of instruments, but you'll need to make sure you have enough stage space for other things too! Choose a few new songs and a few old favourites. Make sure you include non-confessional songs, so that the children are not singing words they might not believe.

Drama

Do you need to adapt the script to fit the number or gender of your cast members, or the limitations of your venue? How much rehearsal time will you need? How will you obtain or make the necessary props, costumes and scenery?

Training

How, and when, will you train your leaders? See Part 3, page 20.

Craft

Where will you get the necessary materials and equipment? Do you need to ask your congregation to collect particular items (such as junk for the junk modelling)? A dedicated craft team can be very useful, especially in the run-up to CHAMPION'S CHALLENGE. This team should collect the necessary materials etc. They'll also be able to make templates and patterns for the children to draw around or cut out. The craft team should make up prototypes of the crafts, and pass on any hints to the children's group leaders.

Involve local schools in amassing reusable material to use during the week (glass jars, plastic bottles, travel magazines for collage, etc.) This gets people actively contributing to the club before it has begun, including the children!

Data protection

How will you maintain the confidentiality of the

information you receive on the registration forms? Make sure your church is registered under the Data Protection Act. Visit www.informationcommissioner.gov.uk and click on 'Data protection'.

Games

Consider what games you can play based on the number of children, your venue and the equipment you have. Make sure you have all the equipment you need.

Accidents

Make sure you have at least one person appointed as a first-aider with a current first aid certificate and access to an up-to-date first aid kit. The whole team should know who is responsible for first aid. You will also need an accident book to record any incidents. This is essential in the event of an insurance claim. The matter should be recorded, however small, along with details of the action taken. For other health and safety information visit www.rospa.co.uk

Fire procedures

It is essential that the whole team knows emergency procedures, including fire exits and assembly points, and where to access a telephone in case of emergency. Ensure you keep all fire exits clear.

Prayer team

Make sure you have a team of people committed to prayer throughout the preparation and the club itself. Keep the whole church well informed too. The prayer team should keep on praying for the children in the club in the months after CHAMPION'S CHALLENGE finishes.

Use of the Bible

One of the aims of CHAMPION'S CHALLENGE is to help children read the Bible for themselves. So each day during 'Time out', when you move on to discussing the passage, help them find it in the Bible or *Matchday Programme*s and learn to look for answers there. Use a translation that is easy for children to read (Good News Bible, Contemporary English Version or International Children's Bible).

Children with special needs

Sport can be difficult for children with special needs – not because they cannot do it (go to the Special Olympics or watch the Paralympics on television and you will quickly become aware of how able they can be), but because when competing against more able children, they can quickly feel left out. If we are not careful they may end up simply watching others. Think about it and talk through how you will handle this if any children with special needs come to the club. If you know in advance of a child with special needs coming, talk with their parents about any

sports where they excel, and try to incorporate these or some aspect of them into your programme.

The 'personal best' section will involve some 'special sports', where all children compete from a different perspective (eg sitting where they might usually stand). But sport can be divisive between any children when they feel they are measured against others. Stress that the aim of 'Personal best' is not to beat others, but to be better at the end of the week than they were at the beginning.

Set the scene

Set up the room with suitable decorations – eg posters, sticks, nets, team strips, supporters' scarves etc.

Set up the stage/presenters' area with a waste-paper basket for 'Slam Dunk' jokes. You could give presenters chairs and a coffee table, such as the style of set for presenters on TV during many sporting occasions. But it can be harder to interact with children and keep a degree of pace when sitting so think it through carefully.

Make sure your welcome/registration area is welcoming! The welcome team should be smiling and courteous. Children need to know they are wanted and parents need to know that their children will be well looked after. The area itself should be well marked out, with plenty of space for parents/carers to register the children and to spend a few minutes chatting to the welcome team without feeling hurried out of the door!

Set up the team dugouts. You could mark these out with bunting or old sports nets, and decorate them with supporter scarves, rosettes etc. If possible use a sports bag for each team to store pens, Bibles etc. Allocate a colour for each team and ask each captain to design a team flag. Copy an outline of the team flags and gather collage materials for these so that the children can decorate them during a team time. (There are some sample flags available on the CHAMPION'S CHALLENGE website.)

Fill the screen

If you are using a video projector or OHP, use a default image when it is not being used, so that the screen is never blank. Use something simple like the CHAMPION'S CHALLENGE logo or some photos of sports people in action. The logo and other artwork is available on the DVD-ROM section of the CHAMPION'S CHALLENGE DVD or on the website.

3

WORKING WITH YOUR TEAM

DEVELOPING PEOPLE'S POTENTIAL

As well as being a time of great fun and development for the children attending, a holiday club is also an important time for the adults leading and helping out. Helping with a holiday club can be a big step for people in the development of their gifts and ministry.

How does a holiday club develop people's potential?

- It involves people in the church who don't usually work with children.
- It is an opportunity for people of all ages to work together in a way that may not happen at any other time of the year. (A regular comment at one holiday club from team members is, 'This is the best week of the year in church!' Probably the most demanding and tiring too!)
- It develops people's gifts and lets them take risks.
- It discovers people's untapped gifts and enthusiasms.
- It provides a structure for the overall leadership of the club/church to seek out and encourage people to 'have a go'. (The age of volunteering has passed so don't rely on issuing a general plea for volunteers. Look at who you have available and ask people personally, giving them good reasons why you think they could fulfil whatever task you have identified. That suggests that you believe in them! They are far more likely to agree to get involved!)

AREAS OF RESPONSIBILITY

A successful holiday club requires a good team who work together well, each knowing their responsibility and carrying out their role efficiently. In other programmes these people would be called 'team' – but in CHAMPION'S CHALLENGE that name is reserved for the children! The adult team working on CHAMPION'S CHALLENGE is therefore known collectively as the Ground Staff. Below are some of the key roles that you will need to fill, and some idea of what is involved in each.

OVERALL LEADER

Ideally this would be someone who is not involved in the presentation. Their role would be to:

- Make any on-the-spot decisions such as accepting extra children at the door
- Keep the whole programme to time, moving things on when necessary
- Look at quality of presentation, watching out for problems such as too much banter between Ground Staff and presenters
- Watch out for children who are not joining in well and helping them to become part of things – perhaps taking

them to the 'bench' for a chat
- Being the person to whom everyone would report, in the event of a fire

GRANDSTAND PRESENTERS

These need to be confident, capable people who communicate well and will build a good rapport with the children. They are responsible for the Bible teaching and keeping Grandstand moving to time and with a fun feel to it. They need to be flexible and have the ability to ad-lib should anything go wrong (not that it will, of course!).

TEAM CAPTAINS

The role of team captain is probably the most spiritually significant yet demanding role of all! Their aim is to get to know the children in their team, to make them feel welcome, safe and happy. They need to build good friendships through 'Team time' and 'Change ends', and should chat as easily about Bible truths as about what the children did the previous afternoon. They are in a position to answer the children's questions and help them engage with the Bible. They need to look out for anyone who may be quiet or shy and encourage them to join in; help those who have lots to say, to listen to others; and help the team do the various activities. They also should help the children participate in Grandstand in appropriate ways. They need to achieve a balance between fun and order, encouraging and praising good behaviour. Should any child be disruptive, the team captain should correct difficult behaviour gently, but firmly. In order to do all this the team captains should sit with their teams at all times, being ready to answer any questions, help the children participate and facilitate the children's walk towards, or with, Jesus.

VICE-CAPTAINS

Young or inexperienced Ground Staff should work as vice-captains to develop their skills in partnership with a more experienced team captain. Any who are especially close to the age of the eldest children attending should be given help to grasp what it means to be a leader and not to be there as an 'older participant'.

All Ground Staff should be given training in dealing with children, especially in relation to physical contact and not being with children alone out of sight of others, but team captains and vice-captains especially need to be aware of child protection issues and policies. There is training material on page 19.

CHAMPION'S CHALLENGE BAND

Live music is so much more exciting for children than tapes or CDs, but these will suffice if you cannot find musicians. The band should include a vocalist to lead songs, unless one of the presenters can take on that

role. Songs need to be well taught so that children can join in readily. If a lot of younger children attend, avoid too many songs that have a lot of words; choose songs that are easy to remember. Remember to explain any words or concepts that might not make sense to a child who is not used to church.

DRAMA TEAM

A team of four people should be responsible for the drama. They will need to be reasonably confident, able to project their voices and have an ability to learn lines, as it will be much more effective if the cast are not tied to scripts. Three of them will play children, so you could use young people in these parts. However it may be better to use adults who play the parts effectively rather than teenagers who are embarrassed to be acting. They will need a degree of direction to aid with blocking and pace. Someone should take responsibility for getting together props and costumes.

PRINTING AND PUBLICITY

This team needs to include someone who is capable of using a computer to produce publicity, registers, forms etc. The team should take charge of producing and distributing publicity that is eye-catching and effective, and which gives clear details of your programme dates and times.

The publicity will need to be colourful and should appeal to both adults and children. It should use the CHAMPION'S CHALLENGE logo (available from www.scriptureunion.org.uk/champions) and information should be in a child-friendly font.

The publicity/printing team should take responsibility for:

- Posters and flyers advertising CHAMPION'S CHALLENGE
- Registration forms for every child
- Consent forms for parents/guardians/carers
- Invitation cards
- Forms for potential Ground Staff, including an indication of any roles they would be willing to take on. This should also include the declaration form.
- Notes and any training materials for Ground Staff (although the content may be put together by somebody else)
- Name badges for Ground Staff
- Registers for each team, and lists to be kept at registration
- Signs and notices posted around the site indicating entrances and exits, toilets, areas that are out of bounds etc. These should use typeface and colours consistent with the publicity and include the CHAMPION'S CHALLENGE logo where possible.
- Any extra signs or notes to take home advertising

special events, eg family games event, or reminders for your service at the end of CHAMPION'S CHALLENGE

- 'Personal Best' certificates, if you run this part of the programme
- Prayer cards/bookmarks/lists of daily Bible passages for members of the congregation, to encourage them to pray for the holiday club
- Bookmarks, etc to be given out as part of the final Sunday service

REGISTRATION TEAM

Responsible for:

- Allocation of children to groups
- Checking children in and out each day
- Checking that forms are completed fully
- Keeping a check on team sizes if more children register during CHAMPION'S CHALLENGE
- Ensuring each child is to be picked up or has permission to walk home themselves. If you have a lot of children attending the club, it can be hard to keep track of who has permission to collect which child, especially when parents help each other out. A collection slip, which can be given to the adult who will pick the child up, is on the CHAMPION'S CHALLENGE website.

SECURITY

This is a dual role, ensuring that:

- no children leave the building unless they have permission to do so
- only children and adults involved in CHAMPION'S CHALLENGE enter during the programme

This person must be confident to gently challenge anyone who should not be present and ask them to leave if they are not involved in the holiday club.

Once the programme has begun, this role could double up with registration, but if so, be sure to have someone who covers security as children arrive and leave, to ensure that no child goes home unchecked.

CHILD PROTECTION PERSON

Your church should have a designated person for this role but they may not be involved in the holiday club. If they are not involved, decide who is to take on the role during the week and arrange for them to be briefed and trained as necessary by your church's child protection person. If possible the person in this role should not be involved in a group or in leading the programme. Make sure that all the Ground Staff know who is responsible for child protection during the week, and have been adequately trained in how to deal with any issues that arise.

FIRST-AIDER

Aim to have at least one person with a valid qualification. If possible have assistants too, and aim to have men to deal with boys and women to deal with girls. Ask them to check in advance that your kit is adequate. You will also need an accident book where full details are recorded (eg name of child, accident details, action taken, signature of person who dealt with it and signature of the parent).

HEALTH AND SAFETY PERSON

This person will need to plan how you will evacuate the building in the event of a fire. Check that fire escapes are kept clear, that Ground Staff know the position of fire extinguishers, and know what the fire alarm – or noise that means 'leave the building immediately' – sounds like. Each team captain should be a roll-call marshal for their teams. The health and safety person is in charge of clearing the building and dealing with the emergency services, but they should allocate responsibility for checking other areas of the building (toilets, snack bar, etc) to other Ground Staff who will be present each day. You may want to incorporate a fire drill into your programme early in the week. The children will be used to this from school, but it might help the adults!

They should also make sure all the activities are adequately risk-assessed before the club starts.

SNACK BAR STAFF

This team organises and serves refreshments for the groups at the appropriate time. They must check with the registration team for any food allergies. At least one person in this team should have a Basic Food Hygiene certificate.

TECHNICAL TEAM

The extent of this role will vary according to the amount of technology you use, but their responsibilities will cover the following areas:

- Visual – OHP or laptop and projector, screen, or DVD and TV
- Audio – PA system for presenters and band, CD/tape player.

CRAFT TEAM

This team is responsible for selecting and resourcing craft, including preparing a finished version of each item to show the children what they are making, and providing everything needed for each team's kit bags (pens, paper, badge making, etc). Each day one of the team should explain how the craft is made and supervise the activity, even if it is done in teams.

SPORTS TEAM

This team is responsible for selecting and resourcing games, including the Personal Best activities. They could also lead the warm-up section of Grandstand 1.

STAGE MANAGER

If you have enough people to cover it, this role will help towards the smooth running of your programme, especially during Grandstand. The stage manager should ensure that all props are in place, including the Slam Dunk basket, and any drama props. They should make sure everyone who is taking part in Grandstand is ready to go on at the right time.

Being practical, it is obvious that you may not be able to have different people taking on each of these roles! It is possible to double them up, but where possible involve people who have or can learn the necessary skills so that you share the workload.

As far as possible Ground Staff should wear sports clothing, but this must be appropriate for wearing among children (not all sportswear is!). Some team will not have sportswear or may not be comfortable wearing shorts, so suggest alternatives rather than have people drop out because they are not comfortable in the clothing. It would be helpful, both for the effect and for parents to spot leaders, if all Ground Staff wore CHAMPION'S CHALLENGE T-shirts (see inside back cover).

Get as much as possible of the craft prepared in advance; there may well be church members who, while they can't help at the club itself, will be happy to help with cutting out, etc.

If you are not doing the badge-making activity on day 1 but are using name badges, have as many ready as possible for pre-registered children and have blanks ready for the first morning.

If you have separate areas for the different activities that can be left set up, prepare these: craft area, games area, snack bar, registration desk and the Bench.

TRAIN THE TEAM

However experienced your team, there are two key areas to cover in training: good practice in working with children and delivering the CHAMPION'S CHALLENGE programme itself. Here is a suggested programme for two training sessions. They could easily be spread over several sessions.

SESSION 1: WORKING WITH CHILDREN

Explore the issues on the next few pages. The more contributions from the team you get the better. So for example, if you are looking at 'Working with a group',

invite team members to come up with two key bits of advice they would give to anyone who is going to work with a team for the first time. Write all contributions on a board and ensure that you have covered all the important points. Do the same for the other topics.

Introduce the evaluation form from the website as a way of involving everyone and encouraging group and personal assessment.

Working with a group

• Ensure that you get to know each child by name.
• Watch for children who sit on the edge of the group.
• Never assume that all the children will learn from or experience the club in the same way.
• Make sure that all of the children know they can come to you with any questions.
• Be prepared for incidents of any kind!
• Remember that everything you say is listened to.
• For some children, you might be the only adult who shows an interest in them that week.

Behaviour issues

• Set some ground rules and boundaries for the group – and stick to them!
• Have plenty of materials for everyone.
• Ensure that you have enough leaders at all times.
• Positively reinforce the children's behaviour when they answer or do something well.
• Never sacrifice the needs of the group for one child.

Talking to children

• Think about the words you are using – are they easily understood and do they explain the stories?
• Don't talk down to the children – talk with them! This means getting to their level, physically and verbally.
• Let the children express their thoughts and views on the stories.
• Don't always rush to fill silences while the children think of the responses.
• Validate all responses, either by more questioning or by asking others what they think.

How to pray with children

• Ask the children to name some of the things they want to pray for.
• Break these down into things they want to say sorry for, things they want to say thank you to God for, and things they want to ask God, for themselves or others.
• If you are going to lead the prayer yourself, make sure that you keep to the point and include the suggestions the children made.
• Encourage the children, where possible, to lead the prayers with you.
• Be imaginative in using different ways to pray, eg using pictures or objects to stimulate thought; music for praise or reflection; prayers with a set response;

taking it in turns using one sentence; or prayers using different bodily postures. Suggestions are given each day for praying creatively.

How to build relationships with children

- Be honest with them – children can often see through pretence!
- Be willing and able to share your story.
- React to the Bible story with them; tell them how you feel as part of your exploration.
- Be ready to take surprising responses and comments without being floored.
- Don't pretend to be up to the minute with their lives. Ask them to tell you what's going on and what's new.
- Never be afraid to admit that you don't know something – we are all on a journey of discovery together.

Preparing to work with children

- Think about the activities you are about to do, and allow for the possibilities of mess and difficulties.
- Gather together the resources you will need and have them close at hand.
- Check that the felt-tip pens work and that the paints have not dried out!
- Consider how you will move from one activity to the next.

Reading the Bible with children

At CHAMPION'S CHALLENGE we want children to understand that the Bible is God's Word for them today. It is important that the times when you read the Bible together are enjoyable and make sense to them! Children are not simply reading the Bible to get answers to our questions. Instead, we want their curiosity raised so that they can expect to meet God as they read the Bible, not just now, but in the future.

Matchday Programme is there to help you read the relevant part of the Bible at the club. Make sure that you have a child-friendly version of the Bible with you which doesn't look tatty. (The CEV is the version used in *Matchday Programme*) If you copy out the relevant verses onto paper or acetate, ensure that the children see that it is from the Bible.

- Break a Bible passage into smaller chunks and go over it a little at a time.
- Think of ways to engage the children's thoughts as the verses are read. Help them listen. Suggestions for this have been given each day.
- Ask only a confident child to read out loud.
- Remember that many children find reading difficult, because of their age and/or educational ability. This does not stop them listening or using their imaginations to enter the Bible.
- This might be a child's first experience of Bible reading. Make it a positive one!

- You will need to explain about chapters and verses. Use page numbers where possible.
- Be prepared to recommend a Bible reading guide to follow up CHAMPION'S CHALLENGE

Helping children to respond

Much of the material you will cover in CHAMPION'S CHALLENGE may prompt children to want to be friends with Jesus for themselves. Be ready to help them.

- They rarely need long explanations, just simple answers to questions.
- Talk to them in a place where you can be seen by others.
- Never put pressure on children to respond in a particular way, just help them take one step closer to Jesus when they are ready. We don't want them to respond just to please us!
- Remember, for many children there are a number of commitments as their understanding grows.
- Many children don't have the language to initiate the conversation. Why not tell them during the week that if they want to know more, they can say to you, 'Tell me more about Jesus'.
- Many children just need a bit of help to say what they want to say to God. Here is a suggested prayer they could use to make a commitment to Jesus:

> **Jesus, I want to be your friend.**
> **Thank you that you love me.**
> **Thank you for living in the world and dying on a cross for me.**
> **I'm sorry for all the wrong things I have done.**
> **Please forgive me and let me be your friend.**
> **Please let the Holy Spirit help me be like you.**
> **Amen.**

- Reassure them that God hears us when we talk with him and has promised to forgive us and help us to be his friends. Children need help to stick with Jesus, especially if their parents don't believe.
- Assure them that God wants to hear whatever they say. Give them some prayer ideas.
- Encourage them to keep coming to Christian activities, not necessarily on Sundays – their church might have to be the midweek club or a school lunch-time club.
- Reading the Bible will be easier with something like *Snapshots* – but you need to support them if they are to keep it up.
- Keep praying and maintain your relationship with them wherever possible.

SESSION 2: THE CHAMPION'S CHALLENGE PROGRAMME

Introduction

Make sure everyone feels welcome. Then read from John 1:35–42. This is a well known story in which Andrew meets Jesus and is so excited that he drags his brother Simon along too! Share together what it is about Jesus that excites you and why you would rush to bring children to meet Jesus for themselves. Pray for one another, that during CHAMPION'S CHALLENGE you will have the thrill of introducing many children to Jesus.

CHAMPION'S CHALLENGE explained

Explain the overall themes of the programme (see page 8), highlighting the fact that each day's title uses a different sporting image to explain a different facet of who Jesus is and how the children will discover more about Jesus through the roles of people involved with sports' teams.

You will also want to introduce the challenge to team members to learn Luke 9:23. Teach the song and show the first episode of the DVD, if you are using it.

Go through the aims of CHAMPION'S CHALLENGE

Make sure everyone has a copy of the aims you have already set for CHAMPION'S CHALLENGE (see page 14) and split into groups to discuss them. Are there any other aims that the small groups can identify? This exercise will help you refine your aims and encourage your team to take ownership of them.

Practicalities

Cover health and safety, risk assessments, fire procedures and basic child protection information. If your church has a coordinator for this, they should be able to help at this point. Alternatively, contact the CCPAS or visit their website www.ccpas.co.uk

Further training

Over the past three years, Scripture Union has produced training features to go alongside holiday club programmes. These would be ideal for further training, not only with your holiday club team, but with those who work with children throughout the year.

On the CHAMPION'S CHALLENGE DVD, there is a training feature on expanding your church's ministry beyond a five-day holiday club. Many churches run midweek clubs and put on special holiday club events at other times of the year to grow relationships created at holiday clubs.

On the *Wastewatchers* DVD (SU, 978 1 84427 246 4), the training feature centres on making connections with

the families of children you have contact with through holiday clubs. On the *Pyramid Rock* DVD (SU, 978 1 84427 193 1), the training feature is all about sharing your faith with children.

SU also produces *Top Tips*, a series of books containing practical advice on a variety of subjects. *Top Tips on Handling difficult behaviour*, *Top Tips on Growing faith with families* and *Top Tips on Reaching unchurched children* would be ideal training tools for your Ground Staff.

Top Tips on Handling difficult behaviour
978 1 84427 124 5

A practical and encouraging guide for all those seeking to disciple children effectively. Explore reasons for bad behaviour and enlist your group's help in making your times together enjoyable for all – including you!

Top Tips on Growing faith with families
978 1 84427 249 5

What does the Bible say about families? What can your church do for families? Here's a readable and practical guide which will inspire and equip you to reach out to families in your community. It's packed with practical, fun ideas that will make a real difference to mums, dads, and children.

Top Tips on Reaching unchurched children
978 1 84427 127 6

How do we talk about God to children who know next to nothing about him? Be inspired by some biblical principles on evangelism and find out how to build relationships through natural points of contact with children outside the church.

To find out more about training offered by SU and for any other training needs, contact Alastair Wood on 01908 856044 or trainman@scriptureunion.org.uk

WORKING WITH CHILDREN WITH SPECIAL NEEDS

- Value every child as an individual. Before the start, find out as much as possible about them – their likes and dislikes, strengths and limitations. Then you will know how best to include them and make them feel safe.

- Prepare each session with a range of abilities in mind. Think carefully about working with abstract ideas. These may be misunderstood and taken literally! Have a range of craft ideas. Check that you do not give a child with learning difficulties a task that is appropriate for their reading age but inappropriate for their actual age. In other words, make sure that pictures and other aids are age-appropriate.

- Give all children opportunities to join in the activities. Some children with special needs may have distinctive areas of interest or talents that you can encourage. As far as possible, keep children with disabilities with their own peer group.

- If you have a child with hearing difficulties, make sure they sit near the front and that they can see the speaker's face clearly (not lit from behind). If a loop system is available, check that it is working for the child. Discussion in small groups can be hard for deaf children. Try to reduce background noise.

- Pay attention to any medical needs noted on the registration form, particularly any medication they take. Keep a record of any medication given, initialled by the first-aider and another team member.

- Designate leaders to work one-to-one with children with challenging behaviour. Where appropriate, set up a buddy system so that they work closely with a peer.

- Expect good behaviour from all children, but be tolerant of unusual behaviour. For example, some children need to fiddle with something in their hands.

- Ensure that all the children know what is planned for the day. Give the children a five-minute warning when an activity is about to finish. Some children need to finish one activity before they can start another.

WORKING WITH CHILDREN FROM OTHER FAITHS OR CULTURES

- Don't criticise, ridicule or belittle other religions.

- Don't tell the children what their faith says, nor define it by what some of its adherents do.

- Don't ask the children to say, sing or pray things that they do not believe, understand or that compromises their own faith.

- Value and affirm the positive aspects of the children's culture.

- Use music, artwork and methods that are culturally appropriate. For example, Asian Christian music, pictures of people from a variety of backgrounds, single sex activities where deemed appropriate.

- Be open and honest in your presentation of the Christian faith.

- Be open and honest about the aims and content of the work with teachers, families, carers and other adults involved in their lives.

- Seek to build long-term friendships that are genuine and not dependent on conversion.

- Talking of conversion with children of other faiths in isolation from their families is inappropriate.

- Be committed to the long- term nature of the work, for the children now and the impact this could have on future generations.

- Where children show a genuine interest in the Christian faith, discuss how they can be a follower of Jesus and obey their parents, whilst being open and honest about the consequences.

- Never suggest that the children keep things secret from their families or carers.

Top tips on Welcoming special children
978 1 84427 126 9

Find out what the Bible has to say on the subject of helping children with special needs to know God. Be encouraged and inspired with stories from group leaders and parents, and become equipped with lots of practical ideas for welcoming special children into your church and children's group.

Top tips on Welcoming children of other faiths
978 1 84427 250 1

What does the Bible say about those of other faiths and how we should live out our faith amongst them? What can your church do? Here's a readable and practical guide which will inspire and equip you to build relationships with children and their families.

RESOURCE BANK

4

CRAFT

Use some of these activities during the 'Trophy room' time, choosing the most appropriate ones for the resources and time that you have. Remember, as well as giving the children a reminder of the club, the craft time is ideal for getting to know the children better and finding out what they thought of the day's story.

TEAM FLAGS

What you need:

- A4 sheets of white card/paper
- Brightly-coloured tissue paper or magazine paper, torn into small pieces
- Felt-tip pens/coloured pencils
- Straws
- Glue or Sellotape

What you do:

Prepare in advance a simple flag design drawn onto an A4 sheet of card, one for each team (or use the sample flag designs available on the CHAMPION'S CHALLENGE website). In your teams, encourage the children to decorate the flag together by sticking on the collage materials using bold colours. Once it has dried, you can fly your flag in a prominent position in your 'dugout'. Each child could also make their own smaller flag to take home as a reminder of the week. For these, use small rectangles of paper and decorate using collage materials, felt-tip pens or coloured pencils. Attach to a straw using glue or sellotape to create the flag 'pole'.

CERTIFICATE FRAME

Here are two ways to create a certificate frame.

What you need:

- Either cheap wooden frames or card frames
- Collage materials such as torn paper, recycled gift wrap paper, pasta, leaves, feathers, small shells, petals, beads
- Paint
- Glue

What you do:

If you are using a wooden frame you can buy these cheaply from shops such as IKEA. Take out the plastic 'glass' first and keep this on one side to be put back when the frame is finished. Alternatively, make a frame out of card using the template on page 39. Encourage the children to decorate the frame with paint or collage materials. Explain that the children don't have to depict anything necessarily, but can use patterns, colour and shape to create a decorative design. If you are giving out certificates make sure that these frames are the correct size for them!

ROSETTES

What you need:

- Paper plates 15cm in diameter
- Brightly-coloured or shiny card, cut into circles about 10 cm in diameter
- Ribbon in bright colours about 4 cm in width, cut into 20 cm lengths
- Coloured sequins, beads, sticky shapes or glitter to decorate
- Glue

What you do:

Give each child a paper plate and help them to stick two pieces of ribbon to the centre of the plate so that they hang down vertically to form the rosette ribbons. Cut the ends of the ribbon with an upside-down 'V' to avoid it fraying. Glue the card circle so that it sits in the centre of the plate and covers the glued area of the ribbons. The rosettes can then be decorated using the sticky shapes, etc. You could use the team colours or even make a different rosette for each prize: 1st, 2nd and 3rd.

TROPHIES

What you need:

- Air-dry clay
- Plastic cutlery
- Acrylic or watercolour paints

What you do:

Have a trophy for the children to look at to get an idea of the shape of it or print out some pictures from suitable websites. Invite children to make their own trophy by modelling it in clay. The plastic cutlery can be used to form patterns in the clay. Allow the trophies to dry and paint them the following day. (Do this no later than Wednesday, to allow the clay and then the paint to dry before the end of the club.)

MEDALS

What you need:

- Circles of thin card, 5 cm in diameter
- Gold or silver foil
- Blunt pencils
- Glue
- Hole punch
- Ribbon cut in approx 50 cm lengths

What you do:

Give each child a circle of card and enough foil to cover it. Invite them to stick the foil on the card and then to gently engrave a design on one side using the blunt pencil. Punch a hole at the top of the card, thread the ribbon through and tie a knot.

TILES

What you need:

- A box of white tiles
- Acrylic paints
- Brushes

What you do:

Have some pictures of sport or club logos available for the children to copy, or use the templates on page 42. Encourage each child to paint a tile with a sporty picture or logo using the acrylic paints provided. (Some DIY stores do very good and fairly cheap boxes of 50 white tiles.) Children may like to use the finished tile as a mug mat.

GLASS PAINTING

What you need:

- Glass paints and outliner or permanent acetate pens (available from craft shops)
- Small jars or candle holders

What you do:

Talk about how a big torch is lit at the beginning of the Olympic Games and say how the fire continues to burn throughout the games. Say that you'd like them to draw the flames on their jar or candle holder. Show the children how to use the outliner to draw a design on the glass. When this has dried, the children can paint different colours in the outline using the paints or pens provided. (Younger children will find the pens easier to use.) You may have to let one side dry before the children turn round the jar or holder to paint the other side.

SWEET MODELLING

What you need:

- Ice-cream tubs with lids
- Jelly babies and marshmallows
- A mixture of other sweet items such as dolly mixtures, fruit gums, lollipops, vol-au-vent cases, wafers, jelly rings, liquorice shoelaces
- Cocktail sticks
- Foil sweet wrappers

What you do:

Explain to the children that you want them to create a model of a sporting event using the sweets and other items available. They can do this individually, working in pairs or as the whole team. Show them how they can use the jelly babies or three marshmallows on top of each other as contestants; two lollipops tied together to form weights; the shoelaces for the lines on a running track; the vol-au-vent cases as boats for rowing; the sweet wrappers as water, etc. They may want to use the ice-cream tub lid to stand their model on as they work on it and then take it home in the tub itself.

DECORATED WOODEN CROSSES

If you have someone who can cut these out of wood, make them as symbols of support for Jesus (suggest for day 4). It is possible to buy these cheaply (50p each) – check out a website search engine for suppliers.

PERSONAL BEST

The aim of Personal Best is for each child to improve at one or more sporting challenges over the week. The children are therefore not working to beat anyone else's score, just their own. You may want to include it daily, or just three times in the week. It's probably best to choose no more than three challenges from the list, in order to allow time for other games. There is a page in *Matchday Programme* to record Personal Best achievements.

These activities need a leader per challenge to count/ score. At the end of the week, create and give out certificates for each child, naming the sport in which they have done their personal best. A sample certificate is available on page 39.

SUGGESTED CHALLENGES

Include at least one marked * as these are the 'special sports' (see note on children with special needs).

TIN-CAN ALLEY *

What you need:

• Soft small ball (tennis ball size)
• 10 empty soft drinks cans
• A chair

What you do:

Place the drink cans to form a pyramid. Put the chair roughly 2 metres away. Each child sits on the chair to throw and aims to knock down as many cans as possible with the ball. You can either score the number of cans knocked down after three goes, or the number of throws it takes to demolish the stack.

STANDING JUMP

What you need:

• Tape measure
• A mark on the floor to show the starting point

What you do:

Measure the distance jumped, feet together, from a standing position – without a run up!

SKIPPING

What you need:

• Skipping rope
• A watch with a second hand

What you do:

Score how many skips the child can do consecutively in 30 seconds.

WALK IN THE DARK *

What you need:

• Chairs
• A blindfold
• A watch with a second hand

What you do:

Set up a short obstacle course of chairs. With a leader guiding them, each child walks through the obstacle course whilst blindfolded. Keep a score of how quickly they can do this.

BOUNCE! *

What you need:

• Tennis racket and ball

What you do:

Score how many consecutive bounces of a ball on a tennis racket the child can achieve in 30 seconds. This activity can be done sitting down in order to make it a *challenge.

BUZZ OFF! *

What you need:

• A metal frame connected to a battery, with a hand-held hoop to be passed over it

(You may know someone who has one of these or a small one can be bought quite cheaply.)

What you do:

The aim of the game is to avoid the hoop touching the frame and thereby setting off the buzzer. Score either on the maximum distance achieved before the buzzer goes or the time taken to get the hoop to the end of the frame without buzzing.

HOP ON!

What you need:

• No equipment required

What you do:

Invite the children to hop on one leg for thirty seconds and count how many consecutive hops they can achieve in that time.

SQUAT THRUSTS

What you need:

• A watch with second hand

What you do:

Invite the children to do some squat thrusts (hands on floor, legs straight out, then feet jumped up towards hands) for 30 seconds. Count up the total.

GAMES

UNDER THE POSTS

Ask the children to spread out around the room. Choose one child to chase the other children (two children if you have large numbers). When a child is 'tagged' they must stand with their arms out at shoulder level. They are 'freed' by another child running round them, under their outstretched arms. At regular intervals, pick another child to be 'It'.

COACH IS COMING

Ask the children to spread out around the room. Explain that when you call out certain names they have to respond with an action as quickly as possible. If they are the last to do it, they are out. Name the ends of the room as 'home' and 'away' and the sides as 'tee' and 'hole'. When you call these names the children must run to that part of the room. If you call out 'sprint', they must run on the spot; 'hole in one', they sit on the floor; 'ace', they run round in a circle on the spot, with their arms in the air; and 'coach is coming', they stand still.

Where possible avoid elimination down to the last person as children who are out become quickly bored.

SPORTING CORNERS

In each corner put a large sign with a picture or name of a different sport. Make four small cards of these same sports and fold them in half. Play some music and get the children to dance or jog around. When the music stops they must jog to a corner and stay in it. Read out the name of a sport from one of the small cards and whoever is in that corner is 'out' for one go.

PARACHUTE GAMES

LIFESAVERS

Arrange the children so that they are sitting around the edge of the parachute, with their legs underneath the chute. Appoint two children to act as lifesavers and two to be sharks; the rest of the children are swimmers. The sharks go under the parachute and the lifesavers walk around the outside, while the swimmers gently ripple the parachute. The sharks must pull swimmers under the parachute by their legs, and the lifesavers should try to save them. When a swimmer is pulled under, they become a shark. You may need to have one or two Ground Staff around to make sure the game doesn't get too rough. This game is best played on a smooth floor.

WORLD CUP

Everyone stands holding the parachute around the outside. Go round and give each child one name out of five sports you've selected (eg football, tennis, golf, rugby or gymnastics). Lift the parachute up and, when the chute reaches its highest point, call out one of the sports. Each child with that sport has to run under the parachute to the other side and grab the edge again. Every so often, shout 'World Cup', and everyone (except the Ground Staff, who should keep hold of the chute) runs under the parachute to the other side.

TEAM GAMES

Depending on the children in your club, you could play some team games, such as rag hockey or dodgeball (with foam balls). Make sure you keep the competitive nature of these games to a minimum – children are at the club to enjoy themselves, not to get upset that they didn't win!

Take a look at some games books for more ideas, and where possible adapt them to have a sporty theme. Here are some examples published by Scripture Union: *Over 300 games for all occasions*, (978 1 85999 264 7), *Theme games* (978 0 86201 841 2) and *Theme games 2* (978 1 85999 590 7).

FAMILY ACTIVITIES

CHAMPION'S CHALLENGE offers an opportunity for activities that could bring together family groups from within and outside the church. Ideally these would be after CHAMPION'S CHALLENGE, offering the chance for children and their families to meet up again. They could happen at different times in the year. You might want to run large events where everyone comes at the same time, or pair up a church family with a non-church family to do these events together. Here are three suggestions:

WATCH IT!

Make arrangements to go to a live sporting event. It could be the village cricket match, if you live in a rural setting, or a trip to a major sporting fixture. Include food and make a big occasion of it. If cost is an issue, you could do some fund-raising at your church and subsidise the cost. Often, clubs have special offers on certain matches, giving free or reduced-price entrance to children.

You could arrange a large-screen showing of a sporting event with refreshments, flags and lots of fun. You could do this several times a year, offering plenty of opportunities for families to meet. Try to vary the sport you watch together, not just football!

For details of potential activities, check out websites such as www.thefa.com (football), www.lords.org (cricket), www.ukathletics.net (athletics), www.lta.org. uk (tennis), www.england-netball.co.uk (netball), www. englandhockey.co.uk (hockey), www.worldsnooker.com (snooker), www.englandbasketball.co.uk (basketball), www.icehockeyuk.co.uk (ice hockey), www.randa.org (golf), www.rfu.com (rugby union), www.therfl.co.uk (rugby league), www.britishswimming.org (swimming).

TRY IT!

Ask appropriate people – either in the church or others known to you who have a degree of skill in a particular sport – to run a short session of their sport for families to try. Some sports' clubs run community programmes and you might be able to link in with those. Work out what sports you can offer and then have families sign up for the sessions. Pair up regular church families with ones who have not been to church before. So, for example, if the sport is badminton, have the mum and daughter of each family play against each other. If you are running a number of sports in one location on the same day, have other games available – such as board games, Nintendo Wii or PlayStation, or the board game or DVD of *A Question of Sport* – for those who are waiting. Serve refreshments too.

JUST DO IT!

Encourage families to sign up for longer sports sessions and pair them as above. You might run a tournament for sports such as badminton, table tennis, swimming, tennis, football, etc.

DRAMA: WEMBLEY WAY

Although there are humorous situations in this drama the feel is more *Byker Grove* than *The Chuckle Brothers*. It aims to link into the children's world and so uses realistic characters, rather than larger-than-life ones.

Set in Wembley Way Junior School, it follows the experiences of Jo, Sam and Curly and the school's 'Miniball' team.

CHARACTERS

All could be of either gender; simply amend the script as necessary. A mix would be good.

Jo or Joe – rather bossy and quite good at sport. In script is female.

Sam – his/her best friend. Actually a lot better at sport! In script is male.

Curly – has very straight hair. Not at all sporty! Also known as James (or change to a girl's name). In script is male.

Mr/Mrs Ellis – teacher at school who is training the Miniball team. In script is female.

Choose some music to use as a theme tune, so that the children know when the drama begins and ends.

SUNDAY 1 – SELECTOR

Setting: Lunch break in the tutor's classroom at Wembley Way School.

Props: Sign saying, 'Wembley Way School' put up in a prominent position on stage, two tennis or badminton rackets and a soft ball, a pile of books, a notice headed 'MINIBALL TEAM', a whistle

Costumes: Jo, Sam and Curly should wear something that represents school uniform such as a sweatshirt or school tie. Mrs Ellis should be in a suitable outfit for a teacher.

Part 1

Cue music. Mrs Ellis enters carrying a pile of books, followed by as many 'children' as possible. They are clamouring round her excitedly.

Mrs E: All right, settle down children! I'll put up a list of who is playing in the teams after school and if you are chosen we can practise tonight during sport's club. Now it's time you were in your classrooms: the bell for the end of dinner will ring at any moment. *(Most disperse, leaving Jo and Mrs Ellis.)*

Jo: *(Being extra polite and helpful, hoping it will get her noticed for the team!)* Do you need a hand to carry your books, Mrs Ellis?

Mrs E: I'm fine thanks, Jo. I can manage.

Jo: *(Being very polite.)* That was a great session Mrs Ellis – you're a very good coach.

Mrs E: Thank you, Jo.

Jo: *(Not giving up easily.)* So what are you looking for in the Miniball team?

Mrs E: Well, obviously, we want the best players possible, but they also need to be fit – Miniball is a fast game, as I'm sure you've discovered – and they need to have the right attitude.

Jo: You mean they've got to want to win?

Mrs E: Yes, but also they've got to be good losers, and patient people, who don't give up the minute they start to go behind.

Jo: *(Gloomily.)* I'll never make it into the team then!

Mrs E: And then I need to make up teams who will work well together – really be a team, not just three players who are good. Miniball depends on everyone doing their bit.

Jo: Sam and I play well together!

Mrs E: You do, and I promise to remember that. Now I must get to my class: you'll know before you go home! *(She leaves as Sam and Curly enter. Curly is carrying a racket.)*

Sam: What did she say Jo – will we be on the team?

Curly: Will I be on the team? Let me have a go! *(He swishes his racket backwards and forwards so that Sam has to duck quickly each time.)* Go on, try me!

Sam: Are you ready, Curly?

Curly: Ready! *(Sam hits the ball to Curly who dives for it but misses. They repeat this a few times until eventually Curly hits himself on the head and falls over.)*

Sam: Curly, I think you're not quite up to the team standard yet. But… keep practising!

Jo: I told Mrs Ellis that you and I play well together Sam – she must pick us, surely!

Sam: We'll know by the end of the afternoon. See you later Jo. Come on Curly! *(All exit, Curly still swishing his racket and Sam still ducking.)*

Cue music.

Part 2
Setting: After school outside the school hall

Cue music. Curly and Jo enter, both carrying rackets, one carrying a ball.

Curly: Go on, Jo, give me another hit – I'm getting better!

Jo: Are you sure, Curly?

Curly: I'm positive!

(She hits the ball to him and he misses it wildly. He then picks it up to serve underarm, but misses the ball every time he lets it drop for the serve. There is much swishing of the racket, much looking round wildly for the ball, and much sighing from Jo. Eventually she sits down with her back to him.)

Jo: Curly, you AREN'T any better – if anything you're worse!

Curly: *(Cheerfully.)* Oh well, my dad always says I've got two left feet so maybe I've got two left hands as well!

Jo: *(Under her breath.)* Yeah, and two left eyes!

Mrs Ellis enters and pins up a notice headed 'MINIBALL TEAM'. She blows a whistle – at which Curly jumps up three feet into the air, as she is just behind him, and children come running in.

Mrs E: Quiet everyone! I know you want to know who are in the teams – well here goes. Vikram Singh, you are selected for the first team. You will play alongside Sam Wilson. But I couldn't quite decide between Aaron Jones and Jo Bell for the third place. I shall make the decision when I've seen everyone play again. I want all four of you, plus Annabel Fraser and Joseph Campbell, who will definitely be in the second team, in the hall now, changed and ready to play. And then I'll make my final choice. *(She and the rest of the children exit.)*

Sam: *(Excited.)* Come on, Jo – you could make the first team! Let's go and start practising! *(They exit.)*

Curly: *(All alone and a bit dejected.)* Oh. I know I'm not very good, but I thought I'd have a chance... *(Walking off slowly, hands in pockets and head bowed.)* Bye everyone.

Cue music.

DAY 1 – TRAINER

Setting: School hall, Miniball practice session after school

Props: Two rackets, a bucket of balls

Costume: All characters in sportswear

Cue music.

Mrs Ellis enters, speaking as if there are several children just offstage.

Mrs E: Well done all of you – you played really well. We have two excellent Miniball teams here and you'll do brilliantly at the competition next week. Remember what I said and keep your eyes on the ball at all times – don't be put off by anything else that happens, even if your opponent does fall over, Annabel! *(There is the sound of laughter offstage.)* Well I've thought about it long and hard, and the last place in the first team goes to Jo – well done Jo! *(Applause offstage.)* OK everybody – just carry on practising in pairs while I put away the nets. *(She exits and Sam and Jo enter. They begin to hit the ball gently between them as they talk.)*

Sam: Oh Jo! That's brilliant! Will you be my practice partner?

Jo: Of course, I will. Oh, I'm so excited, Sam – you, me and Vikram in the first team! We're going to be brilliant!

Sam: Only if we do what Mrs Ellis has told us. *(He mimics Mrs Ellis.)* Miniball is a cross between tennis, badminton and volleyball.

Jo: *(Mimicking too.)* The aim of the game is to score by getting the ball down...

Sam: ...on the floor in your opponents' court.

Jo: The team can hit the ball between them to...

Sam: ...gain the best chance of getting a score, but...

Jo: ...each player can only hit the ball once.

Mrs Ellis enters with a bucket of balls, Sam and Jo do not notice.

Sam: It must be hit over the net...

Jo: ...by the third player at the latest. So it's vital that...

Sam: ...everyone works together, with...

Both: ...everyone helping the rest of their side!

Mrs E: Very good, you two!

Sam and Jo leap up and the ball is whacked into the audience in surprise. Both stand grinning embarrassedly at Mrs Ellis. The actors should make the most of this moment!

Sam: Er, sorry Mrs Ellis! *(Jo giggles nervously.)*

Mrs E: Now some tips for you both: Sam, remember to keep the racket head up when you go for those shots at waist height, and Jo, keep moving your feet. You want to get into the best position to play your shots. That's it – step back for the deeper ones. *(She throws a ball up high to Jo, who steps back, turns to get the shot and falls over.)*

Jo: Oops!

Mrs E: *(Throwing another ball.)* Keep your eye on the ball, Jo!

Jo: Yes, Mrs Ellis. *(She dives for the next shot and heads the ball.)* Is that what you mean, Mrs Ellis?

Mrs E: Erm…

Jo: Did I play well in the trial then?

Mrs E: You played very well, Jo – you remembered everything I'd said about taking your time and playing the ball into a good position ready for the next person to get their best shot from yours. I've told Aaron that he's got to work harder on that. That's why I chose you, rather than him. Listening to your trainer is so important. But don't just listen – do as you're told! *(She exits.)*

Jo: She sounds like my mum! She's always saying, 'Do as you're told'!

Sam: Yes, but Mrs Ellis does know what she's talking about when it comes to Miniball. Vikram says she's the best teacher for miles around. *(Curly enters.)* Hi Curly!

Jo: Hey Curly – guess what?

Curly: I'm in the team – yes! *(He pulls his shirt up over his head like a footballer and runs round in circles. Only do this if Curly is played by a male!)*

Jo: No, Curly – but I am!

Curly: *(Stopping dead, dejected.)* Oh. Oh well, well done, Jo! Maybe next time…

Jo: Er… yeah, maybe!

Curly: I could be the reserve – you know, if you or Sam or someone else got injured, I could play!

Sam: Curly, you're my best mate you know!

Curly: And you're mine – well, along with my friend, Dave at church – it's great hanging out with you!

Sam: And you're BRILLIANT as a friend!

Curly: So are you Sam – the best!

Sam: But you're actually not very good at Miniball!

Curly: Not even a bit?

Sam: Not even at all yet! You need to practise a lot and listen to what Mrs Ellis tells you.

Curly: *(Sadly.)* Oh!

Sam: But you're still my best friend! Look, I've got to practise some more. Stay and watch. Come on, Jo, give me a few lobs! *(She does, getting higher and higher.)*

Curly: Do you need a step ladder to get them?

Sam: More like a telescope, trying to see them so high in the air!

Jo: Well, you asked for it!

Sam: That one had snow on it when it came down!

Jo: Come on, lazy, stretch! *(She lobs it well offstage and Sam runs back out of sight. There's a yell of pain.)* Sam! What have you done? *(Jo and Curly run offstage.)*

Cue music.

DAY 2 – PHYSIO
Props: Two chairs, white polystyrene packing pieces in a container, a sign with the name of your church (Part 2)

Costume: Mrs Ellis, Sam and Jo in sportswear, Curly in casual wear

Part 1
Cue music. Sam enters, limping badly, being helped by Mrs Ellis and Jo.

Sam: It really hurts just walking – I can't possibly play. *(He sits down on a chair and stretches out his leg.)*

Mrs Ellis: Sam, what did you do?

Sam: I was reaching back for a high shot, when suddenly I saw the menu for tomorrow – sprout and broccoli surprise is my favourite! I wasn't looking where I was going and I crashed into the cleaner. I got my foot stuck in his mop bucket and fell over. It really hurts!

Jo: Sam, what are we going to do? It's only four days to the tournament, and you're never going to be fit enough! *(She trips over his outstretched leg).*

Sam: Aaagh! Especially not if you do that!

Mrs E: What did the physio say, Sam?

Sam: That I've to rest it with my leg up on a chair. *(Mrs Ellis brings one and Jo lifts his leg far too high in the air so that Sam falls off the chair.)* Aaagh! And I've got to use ice packs to stop the swelling. *(Sam stays seated on the floor.)*

Mrs E: Ice – go to the staff room and ask for some, Jo! *(Jo exits.)* We'll just have to practise without you and hope you're better for Tuesday.

Jo: *(Running in.)* I've got some, Mrs Ellis! *(She trips and throws the 'ice' over Sam – use the polystyrene pieces.)*

Sam: Aaagh!

Mrs E: *(Putting 'ice' on his ankle)* There, that should help you a lot.

Sam: But the physio says it will take at least a week for me to be able to walk properly, never mind play.

Jo: It's just not fair! We could have won that tournament – we're a really good team! If only I hadn't made you go so far back for that high shot! It's all my fault!

Mrs E: It's nobody's fault, it was an accident. But it is a shame for you Sam, as you'd put in a lot of time practising. I'm sorry. Come on Jo – time you were in the hall to play. Sam, stay here and rest your leg. *(She exits with Jo.)*

Sam: It's no good. My mum's expecting me home soon. Better get up then… *(He struggles in a comic way – make this last as long or as short at the children will tolerate – before finally exiting.)*

Cue music.

Part 2
Setting: Curly's church group

Put up the sign with the name of your church. Cue music. Curly enters and talks to the audience as if they are part of his church group.

Curly: Oh hi! I'm really glad you're all here. I need your help. My mate at school, Sam, has hurt his knee and I want to pray that Jesus will make him better quickly. He's playing in this big tournament next week. I know it's only a game, but Sam will be gutted if he can't play. My dad says that Jesus makes people better in lots of ways – sometimes through doctors and sometimes just amazingly, like 'Kapow!' and they are healed! Will you pray with me for him?

'Dear Jesus, my mate, Sam – you know, the one at school – oh yes, I suppose you do know! Well Sam has hurt his leg. Oh, and I suppose you know that too. Anyway, it's hurting Sam lots, so could you make him better? And could you do it quick? Cheers Jesus! I mean – Amen.' *(He pauses for the children to join in with the 'Amen'.)* Well – just have to wait and see now. Thanks for your help. See ya! *(He runs off.)*

Cue music.

DAY 3 – TEAMMATE
Setting: School hall, Miniball tournament.

Props: A poster saying 'Wembley Way – The Beast!', two badges saying 'Team Wembley Way', a pen, three bottles of water, two rackets

Sound effects: Bell being rung

Costume: Mrs Ellis, Sam and Jo in sportswear, Curly in casual wear

Cue music. Curly enters, carrying a poster that says 'Wembley Way – The Beast!'

Curly: Hi, how are you doing? I'm Curly, top supporter for my school Miniball team. Do you remember praying for Sam yesterday? Well, you'll never guess what – his knee's totally better and he's playing in the Miniball tournament today! So I've come to cheer him on. I might be useless at playing but every team needs supporters and I can be theirs.

Jo and Sam enter. They are wearing badges that say 'Team Wembley Way'.

Sam: Hiya, Curly – great to see you! What are you doing here?

Jo: You're… you're not actually playing in the team are you?

Curly: No chance!

Jo: Oh phew!

Sam: Jo!

Curly: It's OK, she didn't mean it. And she's right anyway! No, I've come to be a supporter – cheer you on and all that.

Sam: Well, we certainly need it!

Jo: That lot from Smith Street think they're going to win but they're not – we'll show them!

Sam: What does your poster say? *(Curly holds it up for them to read.)* Er… I think there's a mistake, Curly…

Curly: Why? Aren't you the best?

Jo: We sure are!

Sam: Yeah, but… you've actually written 'Wembley Way – The BEAST'!

Jo: Good on you, Curly! We'll be the beast then!

Curly: D'oh! Where's my pen? I'd better cross it out! *(He does so, very roughly.)*

Sam: Good thing my leg's better though – in just four days! My physio couldn't believe her eyes – says she's never seen anyone get better so quickly. She says I'm amazing! *(He turns to practise with Jo at the back of the stage.)*

Curly: *(To audience.)* Erm… I've not told Sam yet that I prayed for his leg to be healed. I'm not sure what he'd say. I think he might think I'm a bit stupid – 'specially after that spelling mistake! Except, he DID get better! Sometimes it's really hard following Jesus! D'you think I should tell him or what? *(He listens to audience's views.)* Well… if there's a chance I might tell him later…

Mrs Ellis enters.

Mrs E: It's time for your first match! James! What are you doing here? You're not expecting to play are you?

Curly: It's OK, Mrs Ellis, I've come as a supporter.

Mrs E: Well done for coming, James. Supporters are

very important. Here, have a badge. *(She hands him one of the 'Team Wembley Way' badges.)*

Curly: Wow! It says 'Team Wembley Way'! Like I'm a proper team member!

Sam: *(Coming back to the front of the stage.)* Well, you ARE my teammate – just not in quite the same way as Jo and Vikram are!

Jo: You'd better come and cheer loud then! *(They exit.)*

Cue music.

Part 2

Cue music. Jo, Sam and Curly enter with bottles of water. Jo and Sam sprawl on the floor at first, as if exhausted, dropping their rackets on the floor.

Curly: What a score! You played really well! You must be in with a chance of winning the tournament!

Sam: Yeah, and only one game left to play!

Jo: Against that stupid Smith Street team – I hate them!

Sam: They're really good players.

Jo: So are we! Did you see that last shot in the last game? I was brilliant!

Sam: You were quite good!

Jo: I was amazing!

Sam: Well Vikram played great too – and I wasn't so bad! It's all about being a team, isn't it? Just one of us can't win it, not on our own.

Jo: I like team sports – they're great! Did you see that serve I did in the first game, when that girl ran too fast for it and got tangled up in the net? That was really funny! If only those stupid Smith Street players would make a mess like that! *(She gets up and leaves.)*

Sam: Did I play OK, Curly?

Curly: Yeah – OK!

Sam: What, only OK?

Curly: No, I mean, you were great!

Sam: When? What did I do?

Curly: Oh, you did a great smash when that boy hit a really high shot. I thought you were going to fall over! That would have been really funny! *(He sees Sam's look of fury.)* NOT!

Sam: Yeah, it was a bit like that one last week, when I hurt my knee – I sort of expected it to happen all over again, but my knee seems fine. It's great!

Curly: *(Speaking rather quietly and hesitantly.)* Actually,

I wanted to tell you, I, er, I prayed and asked Jesus to make it better!

Sam: You did what?!

Curly: I prayed and asked Jesus to heal you, like he did people in the Bible. And – well, I don't know if it was Jesus or the physio, but something worked because you're fine now, aren't you?

Sam: I am – and you reckon Jesus did it? No way! *(Jo enters quietly.)*

Curly: I'm just saying – I asked him to, and you're better. Funny isn't it?

Mrs Ellis enters, looking cross.

Mrs E: I've just had a complaint from Mr Cross, the caretaker here. He's very annoyed.

Sam: Sounds like he's living up to his name! *(The children snigger.)*

Mrs E: *(Shouting.)* Listen! *(She glares at the children and then goes on, in more measured tones.)* It seems that someone has scrawled 'Smith Street are stupid' on the wall outside. And as they are our big rivals, he assumed that someone from Wembley Way wrote it. Well?

Curly is shocked. Sam glances at Jo, who looks away guiltily.

I'm waiting… If nobody owns up then we will be disqualified from the tournament, so I'll ask again. Did one of you write it?

Cue music. Everyone exits.

DAY 4 – SUBSTITUTE

Setting: School hall

Props: Two rackets, a bucket and cloth

Costume: Mrs Ellis, Sam and Jo in sportswear, Curly in casual wear

Cue music. All four characters come on and freeze in their end positions from yesterday.

Mrs E: Well? Did one of you write 'Smith Street are stupid' on the wall outside? *(Jo and Sam snigger.)* It's not funny!! The person responsible must go with Mr Cross now and clean it off – and do a litter pick-up for the rest of the afternoon – which means not being able to play another match. So we're out of the tournament. And if nobody owns up we're going to be disqualified. Either way, whoever did it has just lost us a great opportunity to win this tournament – we were ahead!

Sam: But that's not fair! It wasn't us, was it? *(He looks*

round, but Jo is looking away.) We wouldn't do that – it's just not right. We want to show we're the best by winning, not by cheap tricks like that.

Mrs E: Well the culprit must be found or we're out of the tournament! So who did it? I'm waiting…

Curly: (Quietly.) It was me, Mrs Ellis. I'll go and see Mr Cross, and apologise and clean it off. Everybody will be able to play the last match. (He leaves.)

Sam: Curly?! I don't believe it!

Mrs E: I must admit I'm surprised, I didn't think he did things like that. Well at least he was honest and owned up quickly.

Jo: And we're still in with a chance!

Mrs E: That's true; come on you two, you're playing again in five minutes. Let's go and get Vikram – and get ready for the match. (They exit, but Jo leaves her racket behind. She re-enters to fetch it as Curly comes on at the other side with a bucket and cloth.)

Jo: Curly!

Curly: Why did you do it, Jo?

Jo: What do you mean?

Curly: You wrote on the wall, didn't you? I could see it on your face – you looked so guilty!

Jo: You did it – you told Mrs Ellis you did!

Curly: I told her I did so nobody would miss the match and you could still win the tournament. But it was you, wasn't it, Jo?

Jo: So what if it was? I want us to win, and it's time someone taught that Smith Street lot a lesson. I thought it might put them off. I want us to WIN!

Curly: (Quietly.) Well, you go and do that then, Jo. See you. (He exits.)

Jo: (With mock bravado, shouting after him) I'll do it. I'll win us this tournament. You'll see. (Pause.) Oh! You won't see: you'll be cleaning up my mess! (She walks off in the other direction.)

Cue music.

DAY 5 – WINNER

Setting: School grounds

Props: full rubbish sack, mobile phone

Costume: Mrs Ellis in sportswear, Curly in casual wear

Cue music. Curly enters, carrying a full rubbish sack.

Curly: Oh! I'm really tired. (He flops down on the floor.)

I've just spent half the afternoon picking up litter round this place. Do you remember? Someone wrote 'Smith Street are stupid' on the wall – I think it was Jo. And then Mr Cross, the caretaker, threatened to disqualify our team if no one owned up. Well, I didn't want us to lose the Miniball final because of that, so I said I did it. It took ages to get the writing off the wall, and this is the third sack of litter that I've filled. I suppose you think I'm stupid, saying it was me. Well I guess it was a bit daft, but at the time it seemed the right thing to do. Perhaps I'd better ring my dad and tell him before Mrs Ellis gets a chance to. He's going to be mad with me, saying I did something when I didn't. (He gets out a phone, starts to dial a number and then stops.) Oh I really don't want to tell him what I've done. Perhaps I'd better pray before I talk to him! 'Dear Jesus, I'm not sure I've done the right thing but please help Dad to understand and not be disappointed in me. Amen.'

Phew! Now for Dad. (He carries on dialling a number and waits a moment.) Hi Dad, it's me. Dad, you might be cross with me, but… (He walks slowly offstage as he says this, and walks back, still speaking.) Really? And you think what I've done is a bit like that? Amazing! Bye, Dad, and thanks! (He put the mobile away.) Wow! Dad wasn't mad with me, and he says it's a bit like how Jesus stepped in and took the punishment for something somebody else did. Well, I don't REALLY think litter-picking is like what Jesus did, but – hey! Dad says he's proud of me, not mad with me! Amazing!

Mrs Ellis enters.

Mrs E: How have you got on, James?

Curly: I've filled three sacks and the wall is clean.

Mrs E: It wasn't you who wrote on the wall, was it, James? That's not like you.

Curly: (Slowly and quietly.) No, Mrs Ellis, it wasn't. But – well, somebody had to clean it off, and I just wanted to help them to win. Did they?

Mrs E: They'll announce it any time now. You're a very honest boy, James, and very loyal to your friends. I think you're the winner here today!

Curly: I feel like a real loser!

Mrs E: Come on, let's find out who's won the tournament. (They exit.)

Cue music.

SUNDAY 2 – CHAMPION

Setting: Assembly at school hall

Props: Sign saying 'applause', a medal or trophy,

Sound effects: quiet music

Costume: Sam, Jo and Curly in matching sweatshirts, Mrs Ellis in suitable outfit for teacher

Cue music. All enter. Sam, Jo and Curly sit cross-legged on the floor in a row immediately in front of the audience, with backs to them. If possible, have them in matching sweatshirts, as if in school, and play the end of a song that might be sung in assembly. Mrs Ellis sits down until the song has ended and then comes to the front as if giving out a notice.

Mrs E: Now children, as you know it was the Miniball tournament on Saturday. Our teams did very well, and our second team came second in their division. Well done Annabel, Joseph and Aaron. Let's give them a big clap. *(Hold up applause sign.)* And our first team of Vikram Singh, Jo Bell and Sam Wilson, played extremely well and won every match, so they are the champions! *(Big applause – hold up applause sign.)* And player of the tournament goes to – Sam Wilson! Come up Sam! *(Sam goes up and is given a medal or trophy, before returning to his seat.)* Well played all of you. And of course as you go to the High School next term, we'll be looking for a new team to win back the Miniball trophy next year, so everyone else had better start practising now! Now there is one other person I'd like to mention, and that's James Hare.

Sam: Hey, Curly!

Mrs E: James – or Curly, as I think his friends call him – came to the tournament to support the teams, and showed remarkable loyalty and kindness. *(There is a buzz of interest among everyone – get leaders asking the children round them, 'What do you think she means?')* James wins six house points for his house, and I think we should give him a very big clap too, for being a different kind of champion. *(Everyone does.)* Now children – sit up straight please. Class 6, you can leave first. *(Quiet music is played in the background, and Jo, Sam and Curly stand up.)*

Jo: Player of the tournament, Sam, well done!

Sam: Wow! I thought Vikram was better than me. But what about you, Curly – what did she mean? *(Jo looks worried.)*

Curly: I, er, I think she was pleased I'd gone to support the school. *(There is an embarrassing silence.)*

Jo: *(Quietly.)* She was talking about Curly doing all that cleaning up when he hadn't written on the wall.

Curly keeps opening his mouth to speak from here on but Jo is too quick for him each time. Make a big thing of this.

Sam: But you said you did it, Curly!

Jo: He didn't: it was me.

Sam: Not Curly?

Jo: No, I did it.

Sam: But Curly said—

Jo: It was me who wrote on the wall.

Sam: Why? And Curly, why did you say you did it?

Jo: So that we wouldn't miss the chance to win the tournament. He really was our best supporter – he did everything he could so it would work out right for us. Curly, I'm sorry – I shouldn't have done it anyway, and I should have told Mrs Ellis the truth. You're a really good friend! Maybe I should tell her now that it was me.

Curly: Oh, do I get to talk at last?! She's worked out that it wasn't me – that's why she said what she did. But she doesn't know who did write it. It would be really good to be honest with her, Jo. She'd like that.

Jo: I'm going to. Wish me luck!

Curly: Good luck, Jo!

Sam: I thought you believed in Jesus?

Curly: I do.

Sam: So why are you wishing her good luck? Shouldn't you pray for her?

Curly: Oops – you're right. OK, 'Jesus: make Jo brave'.

Jo: 'And don't let Mrs Ellis be too cross!'

Curly: You prayed, Jo!

Jo: Did I?

Curly: Yep – I heard you. You just talked to God.

Sam: You really do believe this Jesus stuff works, don't you?

Curly: Yep. Well he's done some great stuff for me – you want to try him some time!

Sam: I just might. Come on, Jo – we're a team. We'll all go: you, me and Curly. Champions together!

Cue music.

BIBLE DISCOVERY NOTES

DAY 1: TRAINER

Premier aims: To help the children settle into the club; to teach the importance of the Bible and the wisdom of hearing and obeying what Jesus says.

Premier passage: Luke 6:46–49

Older children: Matchday Programme pages 8 to 10

Read Luke 6:46–49 together from page 8, and make sure all the group knows what is going on in Jesus' story. If you think you have a dramatic group, you might want to re-enact the story – you could even update it!

On page 9, think about all the things Jesus says are wise and foolish and write them under the correct builder. Chat together about why the things are wise and foolish.

Using page 10, chat about the instructions Jesus might want us to follow and how we might obey them. Write these on the brick of the house on page 10.

Younger children: Team Sheet from page 54

Read out loud from the Bible this story from Luke 6:46–49. Using the Team Sheet, think about all the things Jesus says are wise and foolish and write them under the correct builder. Crack the code to see who is wise and foolish. Be ready to talk to the children about what this story means to you.

With all children

Explore the story by adapting the questions and discussion starters below to suit your groups:

- Talk about what makes a good house. Why is it important to have good foundations?
- What made the builders wise and foolish?
- What makes us wise or foolish? We should be listening to what Jesus says and obeying him. You would be foolish not to listen to Jesus at all, but Jesus is saying here that it's worse to listen to him and then ignore what he says, because you have heard great instructions for life, but ignored them.
- How can we hear what Jesus has to say? Be ready to share some of your own experiences.
- What does it mean to follow Jesus' instructions? Gather together some suggestions of what this might mean in the lives of your group.

DAY 2: PHYSIO

Premier aims: To help the children grasp who Jesus is, and that as God's Son, everything made by God – even sick bodies – has to obey him. To explain the meaning of faith.

Premier passage: Luke 7:1–10

Older children: Matchday Programme pages 11 to 13

Think about some things that might be impossible and get some suggestions from the group. Ask everyone to think of one more impossible thing and write it in the speech bubble on page 11. Read the Bible story on page 12 together. As you do so, ask the group to think about the emotions of all the different characters in the story. Help the group explore the story by doing the action activity on page 13.

Younger children: Team Sheet from page 59

Do the maze on the Team Sheet. The children should be frustrated that they can't get back to the house. Read the Bible passage out loud and ask the children to listen to it. Do they now know why they couldn't get back to the officer's house? They didn't need to! Answer the two questions and then finish with the prayer activity.

With all children

Explore the story by adapting the questions and discussion starters below to suit your groups:

- What is it like for someone you love to be ill? (Be sensitive when talking about this issue.)
- Why did Jesus agree to help the man? You may need to explain that the officer wasn't Jewish and so would not normally expect Jesus to help him.
- What would you have thought if you were one of the army officer's friends in verse 6? Would you have been surprised when the officer told you what to say to Jesus?
- What do you make of the word faith? A description is on page 13 of *Matchday Programme*. Did the officer show faith?
- What impression do you have about Jesus' power now? (You could use pages 13 and 14 of *Matchday Programme* to explore this further, or read Luke 8:22–25 from the Bible.)

DAY 3: TEAMMATE

Premier aims: To show that Jesus had lots of people on his team and each one had a part to play. It is the same today: everyone who follows Jesus has a special job to do for him.

Premier passage: Luke 9:1–6, 10–17

Older children: Matchday Programme pages 16 to 22

There is a lot of material this week, so you'll need to be selective about what you cover. On page 16, fill the suitcase with what you might want to take on holiday with you. Then read Luke 9:1–6 from page 17, underlining everything that the disciples shouldn't take with them. Talk about how the disciples were provided for and how they didn't need anything that the children put in their suitcases! Explain that everyone worked together as a team.

Go on to read Luke 9:10–17 from page 21 and fill in the gaps on page 22 to help the group become familiar with the story. Get a pitta bread and challenge the group to divide it into as many portions as they can. Would their portions fill someone up? Read the story again, thinking about how powerful Jesus was to make that food go round. Look, too, at the part the disciples played.

Younger children: Team Sheet from page 64

Use the pitta bread example above before you read Luke 9:10–17 to the children. Find the ten hidden loaves in the picture on the Team Sheet. As you do so, chat about what the children think of the story. How did the disciples work as a team with Jesus? Use the discussion to fill in the fish with a word that describes Jesus for the children. Use these words in your prayer time. You could use this prayer:

'Thank you Jesus that you are _____. Thank you that you provided for all those people. Amen.'

With all children

Explore the story by adapting the questions and discussion starters below to suit your groups:

- Can you imagine travelling around without any belong- ings at all, relying on what other people give you?
- Jesus gave power to the disciples to do his work and tell people about him. They were his team! How must they have felt when they healed people, just as Jesus did? How can we be in Jesus' team now?
- When the disciples saw Jesus feed all those people, what did they think of him? Think of some words that must have gone through their heads. Which of these words match your opinion of Jesus?

DAY 4: SUBSTITUTE

Premier aims: To understand that Jesus had done nothing wrong but was killed because the leaders were jealous of him. They didn't like him telling them they weren't doing things God's way. God used this to do something amazing…

Premier passage: Luke 22:47–53; 23

Older children: Matchday Programme pages 30 to 36

Review what the children have found out so far about Jesus. Then go on to read Luke 22:47–53 (on page 30). Talk about how the disciples must have felt and then fill in the faces on page 31. The story of Jesus' trial and death is a long one, so practise how you will retell this beforehand. As you retell the story, hand round objects, such as a piece of purple cloth, a hammer, a piece of wood or a cross and a sign saying 'King of the Jews' at the appropriate times.

Answer the questions on page 36 to review the story and then ask the children their opinion on the story –be ready to give your opinion too!

Younger children: Team Sheet from page 70

Introduce Luke 22:47–53 and then read it out loud. Together, fill in the faces of the disciples on the Team Sheet, according to how they might have felt. Retell Luke 23 as above. Be selective about what you say, so that you don't upset sensitive children, and don't make the story too long. Chat together about what the story means, and tell the children a little about what it means to you. Crack the code on the Team Sheet to find out what happened next.

With all children

Explore the story by adapting the questions and discussion starters below to suit your groups:

- Have you ever been betrayed by a friend? How did it feel?
- Even though Jesus was in pain, how did he go on showing his love and care for other people?
- How would you have felt if you'd been there? The same as the people in Luke 23:48?
- Do you think it was fair that Jesus died? Had he done anything wrong?
- Talk a little about why Jesus died: we have all done things wrong and someone had to take the blame for that – that's only fair. Even though Jesus had done nothing wrong, he was punished for all the wrong we've ever done. He did that because he loves us.

• Talk about what Jesus' death means to you. Talk in terms that the children will understand and be honest and clear in what you say. Be ready to answer any questions the children may have.

• Thank Jesus that his death was all part of the plan to bring us new life.

DAY 5: WINNER

Premier aims: To ensure the children know that Jesus came alive again, and is alive today!

Premier passage: Luke 24:1–35

Older children: Matchday Programme pages 37 to 41

Talk about any surprises that the children have had; let everyone give an example. Vote on whose was the biggest surprise. Read Luke 24:1–12 together (from page 37) and list on a sheet of paper all the things that would have surprised the women. Do the wordsearch on page 40 and discover what the remaining letters spell.

Re-enact the story from Luke 24:13–35 with children playing the parts of Cleopas and his friend, as well as Jesus. Let the other children in the group direct the action. Talk about how excited the two friends were when they found out that Jesus was alive. Talk about what that means to you.

Younger children: Team Sheet from page 76

Do the spot the difference puzzle on the Team Sheet. Talk a little about the pictures and use this discussion to recap the story from Day 4. Read Luke 24:1–12 and talk about how differently the women felt when they knew Jesus was alive. What do the children think? Retell the story of Cleopas and his friend on the road to Emmaus and then finish the Team Sheet.

With all children

Explore the story by adapting the questions and discussion starters below to suit your groups:

• How could Jesus come alive again? Who made it happen?

• If you had been walking along with Cleopas what would you have asked Jesus?

• What do you think about Jesus being alive again?

• You could discuss some of the questions that the children will undoubtably have. Try to talk about all their questions – one that you might think isn't important could be significant to the child who is asking it.

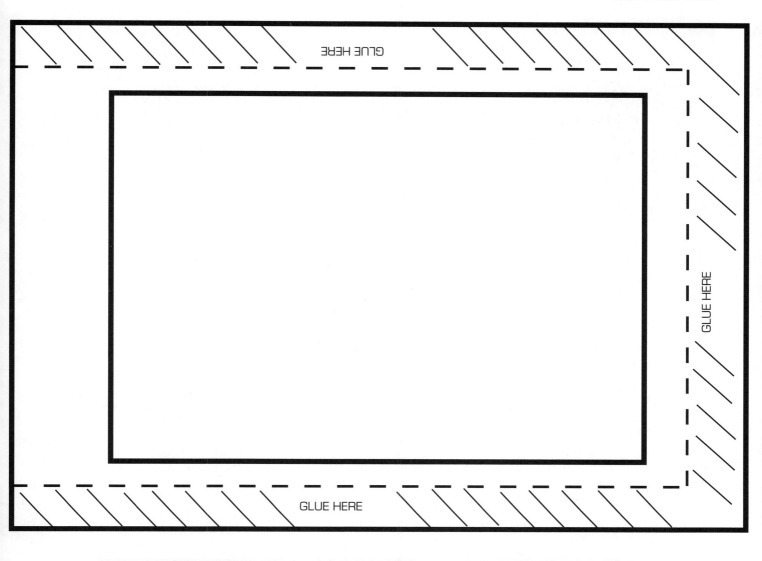

GLUE HERE

GLUE HERE

GLUE HERE

GLUE HERE

CHAMPION'S CHALLENGE

This is to certify that

----

has achieved their personal best in

_____

_____

Club Organiser

CHAMPION'S CHALLENGE REGISTRATION FORM *(Please use a separate form for each child.)*

Champion's Challenge will take place at:

from: to: Please fill in this form to book a place for your child.

Child's full name	Sex: **M/F**

Date of birth	School

Please register my child for Champion's Challenge	Parent's/Guardian's signature

Parent's/Guardian's full name

Address

Phone number

I give permission for my child's and my details to be entered on the church database.   **Yes/No**

CHAMPION'S CHALLENGE CONSENT FORM *(Please use a separate form for each child.)*

Child's full name

Address

Emergency contact name	Phone number

GP's name	GP's phone number

Any known allergies or conditions

I confirm that the above details are complete and correct to the best of my knowledge.

In the unlikely event of illness or accident, I give permission for any appropriate first aid to be given by the nominated first-aider. In an emergency, and if I cannot be contacted, I am willing for my child to be given hospital treatment, including anaesthetic if necessary. I understand that every effort will be made to contact me as soon as possible.

Signature of parent/guardian: Date:

Shuttlecock template

Templates of sports and club logos

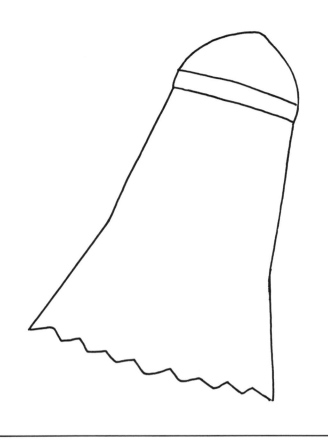

Medal template

Come on you Champions

Words and Music by Ruth Wills

5 DAY BY DAY

PLANNING YOUR SESSION

When you come to plan each day, make sure you have read the descriptions of the programme in Part 1. Select the activities according to the children you are likely to have at the club. Use the evaluation form on the website at the end of each session to identify areas that might not be working well and to get ideas on how to change those areas.

You do not need to include all the activities listed here in your programme.

MAKING YOUR CHOICE

There are many factors which will influence your choice of activities:

- The children involved. The children should be the most important consideration when choosing the daily activities. Children respond differently to the same activity. Team captains in particular should bear this in mind when planning their 'Team time'.
- The length of the club. Simply, if you have a long club, then you will be able to do more! The timings given are merely guidelines; different children will take different lengths of time to complete the same activity. Be flexible in your timings, judge whether it would be more valuable to complete an activity, even though it may be overrunning, rather than cut it short and go on to the next activity. Have something in your programme you can drop if things overrun.
- The leaders available. Not every club will be able to find leaders with the necessary skills to fulfil every requirement. If you can't find anyone with a Basic Food Hygiene Certificate, you will have to limit the refreshments you can provide. If you don't have musicians, then you'll have to rely on backing tracks or miss out the singing. If you don't have anyone dramatic, you might have to miss out the drama.

To help team captains prepare for the 'Team time', the questions for each day are called **Bible discovery notes** and can be found on pages 36 to 38.

Helpful symbols

Throughout the book, you will see these two symbols:

 GRANDSTAND

This logo indicates that all the children are together to do these activities.

 TEAM TIME

This logo indicates that these activities are to be done in teams.

SUNDAY SERVICE 1

SELECTOR

PREMIER PASSAGE
Luke 6:12–16

PREMIER THEME
Jesus chooses his disciples. All are there for a reason.

PREMIER AIMS
To launch CHAMPION'S CHALLENGE; to introduce Jesus as God's Son who chooses a team to work with him; to help the whole church to have an understanding of what is happening this week (if this is your regular Sunday service).

TODAY'S THEME AND THE WORLD OF A CHILD
Children will be very familiar with the concept of selecting teams. In school it happens when teachers select teams to work together in class, or when people are selected for a sports team, but the children themselves will pick teams for impromptu games in the playground. Their team selection is usually based on who is the best, and many will be familiar with the fear that they will be left until last. So it should be encouraging to discover that some whom Jesus selected were not the most likely candidates!

CHILD-FRIENDLY WORK
Children love to be chosen, whether it is for a team or to do a special job. For this service, involve some in helping roles – try to include those who may not often be selected for jobs.

THE PURPOSE OF THE SESSION

There are a number of possible reasons for running this session:

- To get children excited about and involved in the holiday club.
- To inform members of the church about the club and involve them in supporting it through prayer.
- To bring in to a church service those who would not normally come. (Be realistic: you may not get many to a service at the end of the week, and you are likely to get even less to this one unless you know the children already.)
- To draw in whole families rather than just children.

THE FORMAT OF THE SESSION

It could be:

- An all-age service – either in church or in the place where the club will run
- A section of a church service
- A club session for children
- A club session for families

Decide on your purpose first and then plan the format that the session will take. You may find that no new families come if it is a church service: it is quite daunting for people not used to church. Keep this in mind as you plan.

If it is a church service, and there will be children or families there who are not used to church, make sure that you think carefully about your choice of music. Adults who are unused to church may be more at home with older hymns than modern songs. Try to include some that children may know from school.

Remember to give simple explanations of the meaning of different parts of the service. Use words that can be understood easily.

In order to avoid compounding the idea that church is always asking for money, your church might consider omitting an offering, or at least explaining that it is meant for the regulars!

PREPARATION

For this session, you will need:

- Pictures of sports on acetate or PowerPoint
- The 'Wembley Way' drama team
- Sign saying 'Amazing!' on card, acetate or PowerPoint
- 13 volunteers for the Bible reading
- Items for Team talk 2 (Trainers, swimming shorts, cycle helmet, sign saying 'Selector')

THE SESSION

INTRODUCTION

The holiday club leader or presenters should welcome the people and say a little about what is going to happen during the service. Explain that this is the first session of the holiday club, and so there will be a few things happening that are different from a normal service.

SONG

Start with a lively and well known song about God.

PRAYER

Include a short prayer of thanks to God for who he is, for the people who have gathered together, and for the start of CHAMPION'S CHALLENGE. Ask God to help everyone to know Jesus better through it.

SETTING THE SCENE

Present the theme for *CHAMPION'S CHALLENGE* by showing pictures of various sports on PowerPoint or acetate. Ask people to stand up when they see a sport they enjoy playing or watching. Try to include some minority sports, such as darts, snowboarding and squash, as well as the more popular ones like football, rugby and tennis. Make sure you show sports played at school, such as hockey and netball.

Point out how we are all different, how we all like different sports and all have different abilities, but that it is important to have a team made of different talents, personalities and temperaments. We can't all be strikers, bowlers or goal shooters!

Teach the CHAMPION'S CHALLENGE theme song, using your band, if possible.

DRAMA

Introduce the drama for the week, 'Wembley Way'. The children of Wembley Way Primary School are getting ready for a Miniball tournament.

TEAM TALK 1

Before the session write the word 'amazing' on a large sheet of card, on acetate or PowerPoint, depending on what projection facilities you have. You might want to ask the congregation to shout the word 'amazing' every time they see the word.

Explain that the most important person the children will meet at CHAMPION'S CHALLENGE is Jesus. Through the week they will discover lots of things about him from Luke's story of his life. But it is such a packed story that there will only be time to read the highlights – and today's section is not even the beginning! Here is a quick run through of the opening part of Luke's story.

Luke's story about Jesus begins with an angel! The angel came to tell a girl named Mary that God wanted her to be the mother of his son. *(Show the sign.)* Amazing! Some months later Mary and Joseph, the man she would marry, had to go to Bethlehem, his family's home town, and this special baby was born while they were there. But he wasn't born in a hospital, or in a hotel or even in a comfortable house: he was born in *(Ask for the answer.)*. *(Show sign.)* Amazing!

Later that night this new family had their first visitors – shepherds, who

had been told about the baby by the angel. *(Show sign.)* Amazing!

When he was 12 years old, Mary and Joseph took Jesus to the temple, the most important place where people in that country went to worship God. Jesus got separated from his family, and eventually Mary and Joseph found him talking with the most important teachers at the temple. Everyone who heard the questions Jesus asked said, *(Show sign.)* 'Amazing!' because he understood so much about God.

We pick up the story again when Jesus was about 30 years old. One day in his home town, in the place where they met to worship God, Jesus read to everyone there from God's Word. It was about someone who would come from God to heal people, tell them God's good news, and help them see how God loved and cared for them. Then Jesus told the people, 'This has come true today, here!' The people there said, *(show sign)* 'Amazing!'

Jesus left that town and went to other towns to do just what he had said: to heal people, tell them God's good news, and help them see how God loved and cared for them.

One day he met some fishermen, and said to them, 'Follow me!' They left everything and followed him. *(Show sign.)* Amazing! Another day he saw a tax collector, and said to him 'Follow me!' And he did! *(Show sign.)* Amazing!

There are more amazing things about Jesus that we will discover today, and right through this week of CHAMPION'S CHALLENGE. In fact, Jesus is so amazing that if you read about him every day for the rest of your life, you would still be finding out things that would make you say, *(Show sign.)* 'Amazing!'

SONG

Sing a well known song about Jesus together.

DRAMA

Part 2 of the holiday club drama 'Wembley Way'.

ACTIVITY

Choose two people of any age to be team selectors, and ask each to select a team of three. They can be any age and ability. Once chosen, ask why they have selected these particular people.

Tell them that everyone in the team must complete the task, which is to run to the nearest swimming pool, swim fifty lengths there, and then cycle back to your venue. If you happen to have teams chosen who are actually capable of this, turn it into something that they are NOT capable of doing, such as climbing Mount Everest! Ask how the teams feel about this challenge. Point out that the selectors did not know the task before they chose their teams. If they had known what it was, would they have chosen different people? Thank the people, and explain that the challenge is not actually going to happen!

BIBLE READING

Before the session, gather together 12 volunteers to act as the 12 disciples (giving each one the name of a disciple), plus one person to be Jesus. Read Luke 6:12–16. In verse 12, Jesus should come to the front and sit down. Then, when the other volunteers hear their disciple's name, they should leap out of their seat, rush to the front and join Jesus' squad, sitting around Jesus in the style of a team photo.

TEAM TALK 2

Remind people of the team selection made earlier, and how the captains made their choices. They had no idea what they were selecting the team to do. Had they known, they would have chosen people who were extremely fit, and who could run, swim and cycle efficiently. (Hold up a pair of trainers, some swimming shorts and a cycle helmet.)

What if the task had been to cook a three-course meal for 20 people? (Hold up some cooking utensils.) Ask for some suggestions of who people would select if this was the task. Why these people?

Remind everyone of the Bible reading about Jesus selecting his disciples. Today's title for Jesus is 'Selector'. (Show sign saying 'Selector'.) Jesus selected all kinds of different people to be on his team. There were lots of people who followed him, but he chose 12 to have a very special job: people who would spend most of their time with him from then on.

And this is what their job was to be: they were to look, listen and learn. Either show the words or teach hand movements to illustrate them – hand above eyes for look, hand cupped to ear for listen, and a raised forefinger for learn.

When Jesus healed people, this team were to look and see what happened. When Jesus told people God's good news, through great stories or simple facts, they were to listen and remember what he said. And when Jesus did things that showed people how much God loved and cared for them, they were to learn.

Through this week we will be telling what happened as Jesus' team followed him in all kinds of places to meet all kinds of people. And we will see how they got on as they tried to look, listen and learn.

It is important that, wherever we are we remember to look, listen and learn so that we understand more about Jesus, who came to show us just how much God loves and cares for us.

PRAYER

Ask people to join in the prayer by using the 'look, listen and learn' actions, at the appropriate times. Pray for the holiday club: for the team involved in it, children who come and the families who are touched by it.

If this is part of your regular service, you could go on to use the same theme as you pray for people who need healing (look), for places around the world where God's good news needs to be heard (listen), and for each of us to grow closer to God (learn).

SING A FINAL SONG

Choose a lively, celebratory song.

PRAYER OF BLESSING

Use something that is part of your church tradition, but one that you don't need to know a response to, so that non-churched children and families don't feel left out.

AS PEOPLE LEAVE

If this is a club session, you might want to play some games or make a craft (see pages 24–27). It would be good to serve refreshments at the snack bar and chat with people about the content of the session. You could even play a dice game in groups where each person has to answer according to the number rolled. Have the questions printed on cards.

1 What part of the Jesus story had you heard before? What part did you like best?
2 What part of the Jesus story did you like best?
3 What part of the Jesus story amazed you the most?
4 If you had been a shepherd, what would you have told people when you left the stable?
5 If Jesus chose you for his team, how would you feel?
6 If Jesus said to you, 'follow me!' what would you do?

DAY 1

TRAINER

PREMIER PASSAGE
Luke 6:46–49

PREMIER THEME
Jesus teaches his followers about hearing and obeying.

PREMIER AIMS
To help the children settle into the club; to teach the importance of the Bible and the wisdom of hearing and obeying what Jesus says.

TODAY'S THEME AND THE WORLD OF A CHILD
Children are learning all the time in life, whether through experience, through play or through formal teaching. So they will see nothing surprising in the disciples having to learn things. There is a challenge to us this week: how do we make the Bible so exciting that they want to read it for themselves and learn from it? Their experiences in school, and at home to some extent, mean they will understand that there are consequences to not acting on what they are told!

GROUND STAFF PREPARATION

SPIRITUAL PREPARATION

Read about it
Read Luke 6:46–49 together.

Think about it
At some time you have probably heard this story explained as meaning 'build your life on Jesus'. Although a very worthy idea, that is not actually what the passage is about! That concept is difficult for children anyway; far simpler – and far more accurate – is that the wise thing to do is to hear what Jesus says and then obey it. To ignore it is foolish. The story could just as easily have been about cyclists, one of whom oiled his bike weekly after he'd ridden it and the other who simply rode it, put it away and never did anything to it. After torrential rains, the first cyclist could still ride his whilst the second's bicycle seized up. Jesus tells the story to illustrate that it is wise to know and obey what he teaches, even if it takes effort, as opposed to being foolish by knowing it and being too idle to do anything about it.

Outside this holiday club, what is Jesus telling you right now and how should you obey him?

Talk about it
• Why is it often easier to listen and walk away than to obey?
• How does this passage challenge you?

Pray about it
Pray for each other to be wise followers of Jesus. Spend time praying for the children, the different roles that people have, and for safety, settling in, happiness, etc. Ask God to give you eyes to see how he is at work.

PRACTICAL PREPARATION

- As Ground Staff, spend time talking through the timetable.
- Set up team dugouts with everything needed for badges, flags, dice games, etc.
- Check that all other resources are already in place.

Equipment checklist

- Registration desk – forms, team lists, pens, any information for parents, etc
- Team dugouts – equipment for badges and flags, die and list of categories, paper and pens for jokes, large sheets of paper and pens for questions, team lists, Bibles, copies of *Matchday Programme* or *Team Sheets*
- Presenters – Slam Dunk basket, rosette for winning team, Bibles; scripts, water sprays or buckets of water, bucket and spade, towel, hard hat and handkerchief for people in sketch; quiz scoreboard, quiz questions and running order
- Drama – costumes and props (see page 30)
- Technical team – PA system, acetates and OHP/PowerPoint presentations, a laptop and projector
- Activities – equipment for games and craft
- Snack Bar – refreshments

PROGRAMME

Children arrive and register. Have a welcome team on hand to greet them and take them to their team dugout. As this is the first day, make sure the desk is well staffed, so that unregistered children and parents don't have to wait too long.

 **TEAM TIME**
(10 minutes)

What you need:

- Badge-making equipment
- Outlines of team flags
- Collage or art materials
- Dice

Each team gets to know each other and settles in by using one of these activities.

Badge-making

As children arrive at your group welcome them, introduce yourself, chat for a moment, and explain how to make a badge. Let the children personalise their badge and then make sure everyone is wearing their badge before you move on to 'Grandstand'.

Flag-making

Show the children the flag design for your team and ask them to decorate it with the materials you have provided. If your team has been allocated a colour, remind the children to stick to that colour.

'Getting to know you' game

As soon as possible, once badges/ flags are made, get everyone together and play this game. If you do not have enough time for this, play it in 'Team time' at the end of the programme.

Each player throws the dice and then gives the piece of information that corresponds to the number they have thrown:

1. Name
2. Age
3. Sport you play
4. Favourite team
5. Favourite sport
6. Favourite colour

If you finish before time is up, play a name game: roll the dice across the circle to each other and say that person's name as it is rolled.

 GRANDSTAND 1
(40 minutes)

Play music as the children join the larger group. The presenters should introduce themselves and welcome everyone to CHAMPION'S CHALLENGE. This will include telling everyone where the toilets and fire exits are, and demonstrate the sound they will hear that means everyone must stop and listen for instructions (eg what sound you would hear in the event of a fire). Tell them any simple rules, such as listening when someone else is talking, always wearing their badge, and not leaving the building except when signed out at the end of the day.

Warm up

Lead a workout to music with a strong beat. The children will have fun and use up some energy! Make sure you include movement that can be done by any children with special needs in the club.

Songs

Introduce the CHAMPION'S CHALLENGE song. Sing other non-confessional songs, suitable for use with children who know little about Jesus.

Slam Dunk!

Show the Slam Dunk basket in which jokes are put each day. Today's theme is sporty jokes. 'Are there any sporty jokes in the basket?' asks Presenter 2. 'Yes,' says Presenter 1, and reads out the name of Presenter 2! Tell a sporty joke, such as: 'Why did the footballer on the transfer list cross the road? To get to the other side!' The other presenter should groan loudly after this but everyone will probably do so anyway! Encourage children to put their own jokes into the basket.

Champion team challenge

Explain that each day there will be a Champion Team Challenge – today's is very simple: teams must huddle around their captains and think of as many different sports as possible. Give a time limit, for example one minute, for the teams to do this.

Captains could give some hints but the majority of ideas must come from the children, even if they don't have many. Captains of young teams may give a little more help!

Presenters then take one idea from each team in turn until all have finished; this needs to be kept moving so the children don't get bored. Reward the teams that think of the most with a rosette for their team dugout.

'Wembley Way' drama

Today, the Miniball team is chosen, but there's trouble in store for one member. Introduce the drama, and if you have not performed the first episode, summarise what has happened so far.

Today's training tip (TTT): Trainer

Following the drama, the presenters should talk about listening to instructions. Mime the word 'trainer' and ask the children to guess the day's title. For example, one mimes a sprint start and the other corrects their posture, or gives them exercises to do. Show the word.

Explain that later on you will discover more about the importance of listening to the trainer.

Tell the story

Play 'The Trainer says' (otherwise known as 'Simon says'). Get the children to huddle in their teams. As children are 'out' they must sit down, but can still play (this avoids them being bored). Play quickly and cheer the winners in each team.

Pick up again briefly on the importance of obeying the trainer's words. Explain that through CHAMPION'S CHALLENGE you will all discover more about Jesus, who was like a trainer to his team of followers.

Watch the first episode of the CHAMPION'S CHALLENGE DVD or tell the Bible story as below. If you have children with no church background, explain that the Bible is God's special book, and that Jesus, who lived 2,000 years ago, was God's Son come as a human being.

You will need four actors: Presenters 1 and 2, Billy and Bob. They could either rest their scripts on top of Bibles in their hands, open at Luke 6:46–49, or perform the script from memory.

Pres 1: You can read the story we are about to tell in God's special book, the Bible. *(Hold it up.)*

Pres 2: Only we're going to tell it in today's words.

Pres 1: Once upon a time there were two builders: Bob… *(Sing 'Bob the Builder! Can he fix it? Bob the Builder! Yes he can!' as Bob enters. He should be wearing a builder's yellow hard hat and look cheery.)*

Pres 2: And Billy. *(Sing, 'We're all going on a summer holiday, no more worries for a week or two!' as he enters. He is wearing a knotted handkerchief on his head. He yawns and stretches.)* Both men decided to build themselves a house.

Pres 1: Bob built his house on rock, where it would be safe and firm. *(Bob mimes using a pneumatic drill.)*

Pres 2: Billy built his house on the beach, so he didn't have far to go for his daily paddle. *(Billy puts a towel round his neck and picks up a plastic bucket and spade.)*

Pres 1: But then it got a bit wet and windy! *(Presenters blow hard and squirt them both with water from mist sprayers. If you can get away with it – beware of slip hazards and ruining the floor – tip small buckets of water over them!)*

Bob: *(Wiping his face but still smiling.)* Thanks guys, I was feeling a bit warm!

Billy: *(Pathetically.)* I'm all wet!

Pres 1: In the Bible *(Show it.)* Jesus told a story a bit like that.

Pres 2: A story that people would remember.

Pres 1: About a builder whose house stayed firm.

Pres 2: And one whose house crashed down.

Pres 1: But why did Jesus tell the story?

Pres 2: Listen carefully to what comes next!

Pres 1: Jesus said:

Pres 2: 'Anyone who comes and listens to me and obeys me is like someone who dug deep down and built a house on solid rock.'

Pres 1: When the flood came and the river rushed against that house, it was built so well it didn't even shake. *(Both presenters squirt Bob again, he waves and stands smiling, arms folded.)*

Pres 2: And then Jesus said:

Pres 1: 'But anyone who hears what I say and doesn't obey me is like someone whose house wasn't built on solid rock.'

Pres 2: As soon as the river rushed against that house, it was smashed to pieces. *(Both presenters squirt Billy, who makes as if to stamp off but slips over.)*

Pres 1: Great story!

Pres 2: Yeah, great! *(Pause.)* Sorry, can you tell it again, I didn't quite get it!

Pres 1: *(Sighing, and then speaking very deliberately.)* A builder *(Mimes digging and bricklaying.)* who is wise builds his house *(Mimes the shape of a house.)* in the best place, where it will be safe, on really good land. *(Stamps hard on the ground and then wince in pain.)* Anyone *(Waves hand to indicate all in the room.)* who reads the Bible *(Holds it out.)* and does what it says *(Thumbs up.)* is like that: they are wise.

Pres 2: Yes, I get that: but what sort of things does the Bible say?

Pres 1: It says things like, 'Love your enemies, and be good to everyone who hates you.'

Pres 2: Right. So if Bob here were to obey that, when we wet him *(Squirts Bob.)* he'd say…

Bob: OK, no hard feelings about the water, guys! The ice creams are on me this afternoon.

Pres 1: You see? 'Love your enemies, and be good to everyone who hates you.'

Pres 2: Wise man!

Pres 1: So when we do the same to Billy *(Squirts Billy.)* he'll say…

Billy: Aagh!! I hate you!

Pres 2: Come on mate, it was just a bit of fun! *(Billy tries to storm off but slips over again.)*

Pres 1: Billy here *(Points to him.)* couldn't be bothered to make an effort and build his house in a safe place. He just went for the nearest spare plot of land.

Pres 2: So when the storms came and the earth moved…

Pres 1: His lovely house got washed away!

Pres 2: Wasn't he a silly Billy?!

Pres 1: Anyone *(Gestures with hand as before.)* who reads the Bible *(Holds it out.)* and doesn't do what it says *(Thumbs down.)* is like this: they're really foolish.

Pres 2: So remember what Jesus said:

Pres 1: Hear what I say!

Pres 2: Always obey…

Pres 1: And you will stay…

Pres 2: Dry and happy!

Both: Hooray!

They take a bow and go off momentarily, as a pause between this and what comes next, then rush back on.

Match of the day

Interview one of the Ground Staff about obeying Jesus. Begin with

some general questions like, 'Have you got any pets?' or 'What did you eat for breakfast?' Then move on to ask about a time when they obeyed Jesus and things worked out well. Make sure that what they talk about – both the words and ideas they use – are suitable for children. Keep questions and answers short and to the point. If there is time, let the children ask them some questions too.

Pray briefly and simply for this person, and for everyone else, that all would learn to hear and obey what Jesus says.

Comment that we can trust that Jesus will only tell us good things, because he is God's Son. He is like the trainer who knows what is best for us. The Bible is God's special book for us, and all week we will discover new things from it, especially about Jesus.

CHANGE ENDS
(45 minutes)

Presenters send teams off to the relevant places.

- 'Time out' for refreshments and Bible exploration
- 'Trophy room' for craft
- 'Stadium' for games

Time out

Serve the refreshments and chat together about the club. What are the children's favourite parts so far? Go on to explore the Bible together:

- With older children
- With younger children
- With all age groups

Adapt these questions and discussion starters for use with your group:

- Whom should we obey? (Draw out the fact that it includes parents, teachers, etc – people who know us and want the best for us, and who are people we can trust.)
- Where do we 'hear' the words of Jesus today?

- When do you find it hard to obey what you're told to do?
- Who is like the man who built his house on rock? (Verse 47)
- What is someone like if they don't obey what Jesus says? (Verse 49)

If you have time left, give out paper and art materials and ask the children to draw the two builders and their houses. As you draw, chat about your team's reactions to the story. What does it mean to them that Jesus told this story?

Trophy room

Make a craft from the list of suggestions on pages 24 to 26. As this is the start of the club, you could choose one of the options which is more time consuming and return to it during a 'Trophy room' time on a later day.

Stadium

Begin with a two-minute game that involves running as a way of warming up. Alternatively, you could have some simple running races.

Move on to Personal Best work. Choose three challenges from pages 26 and 27 and encourage the children to try each one. Mark the results in their *Matchday Programme*. Encourage the children to cheer on the others as they try the challenges.

If you are not doing Personal Best, play a simple game that everyone can join in (see page 27 for ideas).

GRANDSTAND 2
(20 minutes)

Slam Dunk!

Sing one or two songs as the children come back to the larger group. Read out any new jokes from the Slam Dunk basket, and announce tomorrow's category (doctor, doctor jokes).

A question of sport (and other things!)
Football scored

Quizzes can take for ever if they are not quick and lively, so keep this one moving. Always be fair in the way you handle answers: although you want to encourage children to get the right answer, and although you want the right answer to come out, it can be infuriating for children to see another team get three chances at an answer because the first one is not quite right! They will cope better if you simply say, 'No,' and tell them the correct answer. And always repeat the right answer to be sure that the children have heard it.

Split the teams in different colour combinations each day so there is never too much rivalry. You might want to develop a catchphrase such as 'Don't fuss!' and have the children join in with 'It's just for fun!'

For today, create a score chart for each team using card. Each card has nine squares, labelled 'A,B,C down the vertical and '1,2,3 ' along the horizontal – (as below).

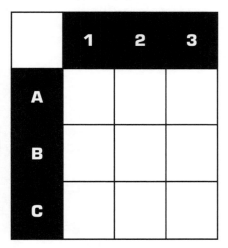

On five of the squares draw a football, on one a goal net with a hole in it and leave the rest blank. Using sticky-backed Velcro pads or Blu-tack, stick lift-off pads on top of each square. If you like, these can have goal nets drawn on the front. Each time a quiz question is answered correctly, the child who does so calls out a grid reference, eg A3 or C1. If a ball is revealed on that square the team scores a point, if it is blank they have no points and if the net is revealed

then the scores for that team up to that point are lost.

Create some questions that are a mix of general knowledge/sport and about the Bible passage.

Champion's Challenge

Explain that through the week you will be thinking about the CHAMPION'S CHALLENGE: the challenge that Jesus gave to his team. Each day you will learn a little bit of it until you can remember all the words. Then everyone can keep it in their minds, think about it, and decide if they want to take up the challenge.
Read Luke 9:23 from the CEV or GNB. If you are using an OHP or PowerPoint then put up the words on the screen.

'If any of you want to be my followers, you must forget about yourselves. You must take up your cross each day and follow me.' (CEV)

Start to teach the *Learn and remember* verse song, so that the children can start learning the verse.

If you want a different memory verse each day, Luke 6:47, 48a would fit well with today's theme.

Prayer and songs
Quickly ask the children what they have enjoyed at CHAMPION'S CHALLENGE and then include those things in a short prayer of thanks. Finish this section with the CHAMPION'S CHALLENGE song and then send teams back to their dugouts.

 TEAM TIME
(5 minutes)

Chat about highlights: what have the children enjoyed most? What can they remember of each section? Finish off any pages from *Matchday Programme* or any craft activities from today. If you haven't already played it, play the die game so that the team can start to get to know

each other better. Team captains should also make sure they know how each child is getting home. As each child is leaving, they should say goodbye and remind them about the next session.

 WARM DOWN

Have a time where the Ground Staff can clear up, tidy things or pack away as soon as children have gone. Then meet for debrief. Ask for any comments – use the traffic lights system (great, could do better, didn't work) to decide if anything needs reworking for tomorrow.

End with a time of prayer. You could break into teams, with each team captain and vice-captain praying for the children in their group.

Finally, make sure any necessary preparation for tomorrow is taken care of.

Ground Staff who have their own children with them will want to get away quickly but do include them in a short debrief and prayer time.

TEAM SHEET 1

TRAINER

LUKE 6:46–49

Wise  Foolish

Jesus told lots of stories about God and how to live God's way. Here is one of them!

Under the wise man, write or draw everything Jesus says is wise.
Under the foolish man, write or draw everything Jesus says is foolish.

Find out what Jesus was talking about!

Use this codebreaker!

You are like the wise man if you:

l○st❖n t□ ■nd □b❖y J❖s◆s.

l_st_n t_ _nd _b_y J_s_s.

You are like the foolish man if you:

l○st❖n t□ b◆t d□n't □b❖y J❖s❖s.

l_st_n t_ b_t d_n't _b_y J_s_s.

Ask your team captain about what this means to them.

a=■
e=❖
i=○
o=□
u=◆

DAY 2
PHYSIO

PREMIER PASSAGE
Luke 7:1–10

PREMIER THEME
Jesus heals people. He has power over illness – even at a distance.

PREMIER AIMS
To help the children grasp who Jesus is, and that as God's Son everything made by God – even sick bodies – has to obey him. To explain the meaning of faith.

TODAY'S THEME AND THE WORLD OF A CHILD
Although faith is not a word a child would use, they understand its meaning and will have exercised faith regularly throughout their lives. From the crying baby who looks to parents for food to the toddler who holds a parent's hand, knowing nothing of where it is going, children show faith – simple trust that does not require proof. So in a sense the harder part is to grasp that this 'man' in whom faith is placed is, in fact, the son of the God, whose creation knows its master's voice – and obeys. Beware: it may sound like magic to some!

GROUND STAFF PREPARATION

SPIRITUAL PREPARATION

Read about it
Read Luke 7:1–10 together.

Think about it
The officer's faith in Jesus is amazing! He is certain that Jesus can and will heal his servant simply because his own orders are obeyed. It shows his discernment that Jesus is God's Son, and therefore everything made by God must bow to his authority. Amazing! We may struggle today because time and again we ask Jesus to heal people who are ill, but it seems like he doesn't. Is Jesus still powerful? Of course he is. But his life on earth as a man was for a limited time, and it was vital that there were many 'signs' about him and his power in that time. So what do you want Jesus to do for you?

Talk about it
• What is faith?
• Does the amount of our faith matter?

Pray about it
Pray that this week will grow everyone's faith. Spend time praying for everyone involved and all aspects of the programme. Pray especially for wisdom when answering children's questions.

PRACTICAL PREPARATION
• As Ground Staff, spend time talking through the timetable.
• Set up team dugouts with everything needed for sporting pictures, etc.
• Check that all other resources are ready in place.

Equipment checklist
• Registration desk – forms, team lists, pens, any information for parents, etc
• Team dugouts – equipment for sporting pictures; paper and pens

for jokes; large sheets of paper and pens for questions; team lists; ball for prayer time, Bibles, copies of *Matchday Programme* or *Team Sheets*

- Presenters – Slam Dunk basket, medal for winning team, Bibles, scripts, quiz scoreboard, quiz questions, tennis racket, at least 12 tennis balls, running order
- Drama – costumes and props (see page 31)
- Technical team – PA system, acetates and OHP/PowerPoint presentations, a laptop and projector
- Activities – equipment for games and craft
- Snack Bar – refreshments

PROGRAMME

Play some lively music and display the CHAMPION'S CHALLENGE logo to welcome the children as they arrive and are registered. Have a welcome team on hand to greet them and take them to their team dugout.

 **TEAM TIME**
(10 minutes)

What you need:
- Paper
- Crayons or felt–tip pens
- Outlines for younger children to colour (see website)

Make any new children especially welcome and ask if any of your team can fill in the newcomers on what happened on Day 1. Any children with items for the Slam Dunk basket should put them in now. Each team should spend time together on one or more of these activities.

Sporting colours
Encourage the children to draw or colour in sporting pictures to decorate their team dugout. Make sure you include a good range of sports. As they do this, chat together about what they did after CHAMPION'S CHALLENGE yesterday, about what they like best about the

club and what they can remember from Day 1's story.

The trainer says
Play 'The trainer says' (see 'Tell the story' on page 51), reminding the team of yesterday's theme. Explain that today's story is about someone who could do nothing – who was very ill and could only lie still in bed!

 GRANDSTAND 1
(40 minutes)

Play the CHAMPION'S CHALLENGE song as the children join the larger group. The presenters should introduce themselves again and welcome everyone to CHAMPION'S CHALLENGE, especially any new children. Remind the children about the Slam Dunk basket.

Warm up
Lead a workout to music with a strong beat. Include movements that you did on Day 1, together with some new exercises. All the Ground Staff should join in and play their part in keeping the energy levels high!

Songs
Sing the CHAMPION'S CHALLENGE song. Also sing some non-confessional songs, including at least one that you sang yesterday. Don't try to teach too many new songs all at once!

'Wembley Way' drama part 1
Introduce the drama and remind the children about what happened in Day 1. What can be done about Sam's injury?

Champion team challenge
Ask the teams to stand up around their team captains; on a whistle blow, they must organise themselves into height order, shortest at the front and tallest at the back. But nobody is allowed to speak as they do this! The first team to do so gets a medal to decorate their team dugout.

Slam Dunk!
Check the Slam Dunk basket for jokes and read out the best ones.

Today's training tip (TTT): Physio
Introduce the Bible teaching by miming a player going down injured and the physio coming on to help them, by moving their leg around and spraying on something. If the children cannot guess what job is being mimed, give a verbal clue. Once they have guessed it, show the word and get them to listen out for Jesus having that role in today's story.

Tell the story
Watch episode 2 of the CHAMPION'S CHALLENGE DVD or tell the Bible story as provided below.

One person is the storyteller while another mimes (ideas are written in italics). The storyteller should have a Bible in their hand, open at Luke 7:1–10.

The mime actor should start off left of centre as they will move further to the right during the mime. You could use lots of people for the different parts, but if done well, it may be more memorable with just one person miming everything.

Have you ever seen soldiers marching to the orders of their commander? 'Left! Right! Left! Right! Left! Right! Left! Right! Atten-TION!'

They have to do exactly as they are told, otherwise it all goes wrong. 'Left! Right! Left! Right! Left! Right! Right! Left! Atten-OW!' *(Actor mimes bumping into someone else.)*

You can imagine the mess if they all tripped over each other! They have to listen very carefully to what their commander says, and obey the orders they are given. *(Actor stands to attention.)*

That's a bit like what we heard yesterday: Jesus says we should listen to him and do as he says.

Well in today's story from the Bible we

hear about a soldier who knew that Jesus was important and powerful – even when he wasn't in the place where he was needed!

Jesus went to the town of Capernaum. In that town lived an army officer. *(Actor waves.)* The officer had a servant, and the officer's servant was sick. *(Actor moves a couple of paces left and becomes the servant. He clutches stomach and mimes being sick.)* VERY sick. *(Same again, twice, but more exaggerated.)* In fact he was so sick that he was about to die. *(Actor staggers around briefly, reeling, and then drops to the floor. Storyteller stares hard at actor.)* I said he was only about to die: he was very ill in bed. *(Actor jumps up and stands stiffly, hands by side, eyes closed, then drops head to one side. Occasionally he lifts his head, eyes closed, shudders, and lets it fall again.)*

The army officer liked this servant a lot – he didn't want him to die. So when he heard about Jesus, he sent some important people to ask Jesus to come and heal his servant. *(Actor straightens up quickly and moves a couple of paces to the right, back to the officer's place. He beckons, points to where the servant is meant to be, then points in the opposite direction; then he clasps his hands together and shakes them as if imploring.)*

The leaders went to Jesus and begged him to do something. *(Actor moves a couple of paces to the right again; he kneels, points back over his shoulder, clasps hands and implores again.)*

'This man deserves your help!' they said. *(Actor points back to officer and then points forwards to Jesus.)* 'He is our friend and has even built us a place to worship God!' *(He shakes hands with imaginary friend; draws out the shape of the building and then holds hands up as if praying.)*

So Jesus went with them. *(Actor gets up, moves further right, turns, and*

becomes Jesus, helping the leaders to their feet. He walks on the spot towards the officer's house.)

When they were near the house, *(Gestures with a hand as if to show that it is near.)* the officer sent some friends to Jesus. *(Moves quickly to the left and turns to face 'Jesus'.)*

'Lord, don't go to any trouble for me! *(Holds hand up as if to say 'stop!')* I am not good enough for you to come into my house. *(Points to self, frowns and shakes hands in front of self, palms outwards, as if to say 'no!')* And I am certainly not worthy enough to come to you! *(Repeats previous action more vehemently.)* Just say the word, and my servant will get well. I have soldiers who take orders from me. I can say to one of them "Go!" and he goes *(Marches away five paces and stops at a halt.)* and to another "Come!" and he comes. *(Turns, marches back five paces and stops at a halt.)* I can say to my servant, "Do this!" and he will do it.' *(Turns to face audience and salutes.)*

When Jesus heard this, he was amazed. *(Actor moves quickly back to the 'Jesus' position and throws hands up in amazement.)* This officer believed that Jesus could heal the man without ever going to his home. *(Peers into the near distance, hand to eyes.)* 'I've never found faith like this anywhere in the country', said Jesus. *(Spreads hands widely, palms up.)*

The officer's friends returned home. *(Actor moves a pace nearer 'home', turns and waves to 'Jesus', then turns back and walks on the spot.)* When they got there, they found that the servant was perfectly well again. *(Actor resumes the 'servant in bed' poses momentarily, then leaps up and down and dances, finally skipping off.)* Without ever being near him, Jesus really had healed him!

'Wembley Way' part 2

Remind the children of where the drama ended and cue music for the second part of today's episode.

Match of the day

Interview one of the leaders who has been helped by Jesus when they were ill or injured, either through a miraculous healing or by the way they coped with the illness. Let the children ask some questions too. Pray briefly for today's interviewee and thank God for the people who help us when we are ill – including Jesus.

Comment that Jesus can heal people because he is God's Son – he has the power to make people well again.

Finally, explain about the Bench. This is a quiet place for anyone who wants to chat to a leader. Announce 'Change ends' and send the teams off to their various places.

◧ CHANGE ENDS
(45 minutes)

If you are doing these activities in rotation, remember to change the order in which teams do each one.

Time out

Serve the refreshments and chat together about today's story – what was their favourite part?

Go on to explore the Bible further:

- With older children
- With younger children
- With all age groups

Adapt these questions and discussion starters for use with your group:

- Why was Jesus so amazed that the officer wouldn't let him go to his house?
- Why do you think Jesus could heal the servant?
- When was Jesus like the team physio in a sports match? What was different about him, though?
- What do you think faith is? (A helpful illustration of times when we show faith is the way we use telephones even though we don't understand how they work, or eat food and have faith that it won't harm us.)

Trophy room

Select a craft from the selection on pages 24 to 26. If you chose a complex craft on Day 1, you may want to carry on with that today. Remember to use this time to chat with the children about what they have heard so far and what they think. Be ready to share your story too.

Stadium

Select some games from the selection on pages 26 and 27. If you are only doing 'Personal Best' activities three times in the week, omit it today.

GRANDSTAND 2
(20 minutes)

Slam Dunk!

Welcome everyone back and sing a song. Read out any new jokes, and announce tomorrow's category (knock, knock jokes).

A question of sport (and other things!)
Tennis scored

Use different combinations of teams for today's quiz. Keep the questions short and uncomplicated, with a mix of sport, general knowledge and today's Bible passage. Ask them randomly, not leaving the Bible questions until the end. Score as in tennis (15, 30, 40, deuce etc), the best of three games. Spin a tennis racket for 'rough' or 'smooth' (make sure you know which is which!) for which team goes first. Keep the score by getting children out to hold a tennis ball for each point won.

Champion's Challenge

Recap the *Learn and remember* verse song which you started to learn yesterday. Or continue to learn Luke 9:23 by writing one or two words on a shuttlecock shape (see page 42), and attaching the shapes to a badminton net stretched across the stage. Divide the verse like this:

If any / of you / want to / be my / followers, / you must / forget / about / yourselves. / You must / take up / your / cross / each day / and / follow me.

Say the verse together several times, removing a few shuttlecocks after each time you say the verse.

If you are using a different memory verse each day Luke 7:7 from today's Bible passage is a suitable choice.

Prayer and songs

Pray briefly, thanking God for the time at CHAMPION'S CHALLENGE. End by singing the CHAMPION'S CHALLENGE song and then send teams back to their dugouts.

TEAM TIME
(5 minutes)

Tell the children that you are going to pray for anyone the children know who is ill. Begin a prayer, and then pass round an item from the team dugout (for example, a ball). If they want to, each child can say a person's name out loud when they are holding the item, or they can just hold the item and say the name in their head, because Jesus will know. Then they should pass on the item to the next person. When the item gets back to the team captain, finish the prayer, with everyone joining in 'Amen', which means 'I agree'.

Pray in simple words such as 'Jesus, thank you that you have power to heal. We especially think of... Please help them, and make them better. Amen.'

Those who are on the doors should let this run to its full time – this is an important activity, and the programme does not end until it is complete.

If you have any time left, go on to talk about the day's highlights.

WARM DOWN

Have your clear-up time, then meet for debrief. Ask for any comments – use the traffic light system (great, could do better, didn't work) to evaluate the day, or use the evaluation form (available on the CHAMPION'S CHALLENGE website or the DVD-ROM section of the DVD).

End with a short time of prayer as a whole group; thanking God for the children who have come and for the times you have had together today.

Finish by doing any necessary preparation for tomorrow.

TEAM SHEET

2

PHYSIO

LUKE 7:1–10

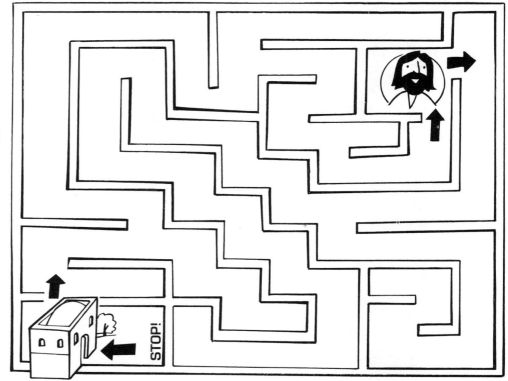

Guide the officer's friend to Jesus.

Then go back home again by a different route.

Why didn't Jesus go to the army officer's house? Look again at verses 7 to 9 in the Bible story and write the answer here!

_____
_____
_____
_____
_____

Do you know anyone who is ill? Write or draw them here and pray for them.

Did Jesus still make the servant better?

Tick the box!

☐ Yes   ☐ No

Thank you Jesus that you care when people are ill. Thank you that you are able to make them better. Please help…

DAY 3

TEAM MATE

PREMIER PASSAGE
Luke 9:1–6,10–17

PREMIER THEME
Working with Jesus. Everyone has a part to play.

PREMIER AIMS
To show that Jesus had lots of people on his team and each one had a part to play. It is the same today: everyone who follows Jesus has a special job to do for him.

TODAY'S THEME AND THE WORLD OF A CHILD
Younger children are not always as good at teamwork as older ones; watch them play football, for example, and you will see that they all pile in to kick the ball at the same time, and have no sense of passing it on to move it down the field. So for them, you may need to explain in more detail why teamwork is good. Even older ones may need reassurance that always being the star of the team is neither possible nor good for them, but as Jesus showed, everyone's part in a team matters.

GROUND STAFF PREPARATION

SPIRITUAL PREPARATION

Read about it
Read Luke 9:1–6,10–17 together.

Think about it
This holiday club will teach you much about serving Jesus as part of his 'team'. Jesus gave the disciples instructions to keep them focused, and to help them rely on God's power, whether it was healing people or being fed! What role has he given you this week? How do you feel about it? For what does he ask you to rely on him?

The disciples learnt lots in their time away but still had no idea of how to feed the crowd that they encountered on their return. Perhaps they had limited ideas about how and when Jesus could work! But when Jesus is there things are always different.

Talk about it
- Jesus told the disciples to take nothing with them. What, if anything, does he ask you to bring to this morning's session?
- What do you want Jesus to do for you today?

Pray about it
Pray for each other to have a very special time today, aware of being a team together. Spend time praying for the day, for the conversations that will happen between children and adults, and for Jesus to be at work multiplying all that is available so that there is enough for everyone and more left over!

PRACTICAL PREPARATION
- As Ground Staff, spend time talking through the timetable. You may want to let team captains come up with ideas for today's Champion's team challenge, in case the children don't come up with anything.
- Set up team dugouts with everything needed for 'Team times' etc.

- Check that all other resources are ready in place.

Equipment checklist

- Registration desk – forms, team lists, pens, any information for parents, etc
- Team dugouts – equipment for team pictures; paper and pens for jokes; large sheets of paper and pens for questions; team lists, Bibles, copies of Matchday Programme or Team Sheets
- Presenters – Slam Dunk basket, team decorations, Bibles, scripts and costumes for storytelling, foam balls in a bag numbered as suggested in quiz scoring system, quiz questions, mirror, running order
- Drama – costumes and props (see page 32)
- Technical team – PA system, acetates and OHP/PowerPoint presentations, a laptop and projector
- Activities – equipment for games and craft
- Snack Bar – refreshments, different kinds of bread (optional)

PROGRAMME

Play some lively music and display the CHAMPION'S CHALLENGE logo to welcome the children as they arrive and are registered. Have a welcome team on hand to greet them and take them to their team dugout.

 TEAM TIME
(10 minutes)

What you need:

- Paper
- Crayons or felt–tip pens
- Large sheet of card or paper

Welcome the children and ask the team what they can remember from the previous days at CHAMPION'S CHALLENGE. Can anyone remember the *Learn and remember* verse(s)? Encourage the children to put any jokes or questions in the Slam Dunk basket. Spend some time getting to know each other through either or both of these activities.

Team photo

Give out the paper and crayons/felt-tip pens and ask each child to draw a self-portrait. After you have admired all the efforts, stick these on the large sheet to create a 'team photo'. Chat about being part of a team: what do teammates do for each other?

Team shout

Work together to create a team 'shout'. You could use a tune the children all know and change the words to make a song, or use a rhythm to make a shout. You might want to work the children's names into the shout, or include some things you have learnt about Jesus. Practise the shout and perform it whenever your team gets together! Comment on how you all worked together to create the shout.

 GRANDSTAND 1
(40 minutes)

Play the CHAMPION'S CHALLENGE song as everyone joins the larger group. The presenters should remind the children who they are and welcome any new children. Ask for any volunteers to perform their team shout!

Warm up

Lead a workout to music with a strong beat. Include movements that you did on previous days, together with some new exercises. Remember to ensure that all children are able to join in.

Songs

Sing the CHAMPION'S CHALLENGE song, together with a couple of songs you have already sung during the club.

Champion team challenge

Each team is going to create a 'machine' that will work together to achieve something, for example passing something round a circle (for younger groups), or a more intricate task of different people bending and swinging arms out (for older groups). This should require real teamwork! Teams have three minutes to create this and then each group has 15 seconds to demonstrate their 'machine' to everyone else.

Congratulate everyone and award a team decoration for every team!

Today's training tip (TTT): Teammate

Introduce today's theme by both presenters standing side by side, arms over each other's shoulders, while one indicates that they are a pair. Ask the children to guess today's title and show the word. Comment on the fact that whilst team mates may often have different roles – such as goal scorer or goalkeeper – each is equally important. Relate this to the 'machines' the teams created.

'Wembley Way' part 1

Recap on what has happened so far in the drama and introduce today's episode. The team learns that everyone can have a role to play.

Tell the story

Remind the children about being a teammate and ask them to look out for ways in which Jesus helped his team in the story.

Watch episode 3 of the CHAMPION'S CHALLENGE DVD or tell the Bible story as below. The presenter who begins this should have a Bible in their hand, open at Luke 9, and point to it or show it as they speak about what the Bible passage says:

How many of you belong to a sports team of some kind? What sports? Do you all have the same job on the team? In some sports, everyone has a different job to do. If you're on a football team, or if you are in a rounders or cricket team that's fielding, everyone's job is slightly different and it's important that everyone does their bit as well as they can. Everyone's job is important, even though it's different from others. It would be no good having a whole team of goalkeepers, or a whole team of bowlers and no fielders!

In other sports, everyone on the team does the same job. So if you're in a swimming relay team, you all have to swim as fast as you can so that the team can touch home first and be the winners! Everyone is equally important, and even though the last person to swim ends the race, all the others have done vital jobs along the way.

When Jesus picked his team, he chose a real mix of people who had done lots of different jobs before they became his special team. We know that some of them were fishermen and another was a tax collector. They might not have got on so well, but they became a team with Jesus.

And Jesus gave them all a new job to do – the same new job. Yesterday we heard that Jesus could heal sick people, and the Bible says that Jesus gave this power to his team too. And then he sent them out to tell everyone they met about his Father God, and God's new way for people to live.

Here comes Rachel, the wife of Thomas. Thomas is one of Jesus' team. Let's hear her story!

A woman enters. She should have a shawl or scarf round her shoulders, or Biblical dress.

Rachel: Hello – I'm expecting my husband back any time now. I got a message to say he'd be back today, and I've been cooking him a meal to welcome him home. I can't wait to hear what he says about his time away. You see he ran in last Tuesday and said, 'I'm going to be away for a few days. Jesus is sending us out to the villages in the area. I'll be back next week.'

'Oh dear!' I said. 'I've just washed your spare tunic and it's not dry yet!'

'No worry', said Thomas, 'Jesus

said we weren't to take a change of clothes.'

'Well let me pack up some food for you' I said.

'No dear, no food. Jesus said we weren't to take any food.'

'Well let me run and ask my brother to lend us some money for your journey so you can buy food while you're away,' I said.

'No dear, no money. Jesus said we weren't to take money with us.'

'Well let me fetch that big stick for you that my dad used to lean on when he was tired,' I said.

'No dear, no stick. Jesus said we weren't to take one with us', said Thomas. 'No stick, no bag, no food, no money, no change of clothes, nothing! But you can give me a kiss, and I'll take that with me.'

So I did – and off he went, empty handed! It seems that Jesus said people who supported Thomas – who were like his teammates – would look after him, and most of all, God would have him in his care. Oh! Here's Thomas now! *(Thomas enters.)* Welcome back! Are you alright? Have you had a good time?'

Thomas: I'm fine, Rachel, I've been well looked after and I've had a brilliant time! I've seen people get better because God's power was at work, and people have been so glad to hear how much God loves them!

Rachel: You must be starving! I've been cooking you a special 'welcome home' meal!

Thomas: Actually I'm very full – I've just eaten a HUGE meal, as much as I wanted, and turned down seconds!

Rachel: Did someone make a meal for you and the others in Jesus' team?

Thomas: Yes… and about five thousand other men!

Rachel: *(Shocked.)* Whoever provided

food for that many people?

Thomas: Funny you should ask that – God did!

Rachel: *(Even more shocked.)* God did?!

Thomas: It was like this. It was so great being in Jesus' team that we all wanted to tell him what had happened while we were away. Everybody was telling their story when we realised that this big crowd of people had joined us. As it got late in the afternoon, we were all feeling a bit hungry. We wanted Jesus to send everyone away to find their own food, but he told us we had to feed them! Well, we checked round to see what we had left over from what we'd been given last night, and there were just five little loaves of bread and a couple of fish. So we gave them to Jesus, and he asked us to get everyone to sit in groups on the grass. Then he took the bread and fish, and looked up to heaven and blessed the food. My job on the team was to take the bread from Jesus and then pass it down the line to James and John. *(He mimes this as he continues to speak.)* Then they passed it to Bartholomew, Andrew, Peter and Jude, and they gave it to all the different groups. I have to admit I was really worried, because there we were passing on this food and I knew there would be nothing left of it for us to eat. But it just kept coming, and we all kept eating, until everyone had eaten as much as they wanted. We gathered up all the leftovers and filled twelve baskets! *(Thomas puts his arm through Rachel's and they start to walk off.)* Do you fancy a fish sandwich for supper?

Song
Include a song at this point to break up the time where the children are sitting and listening.

Match of the day
Interview one of the leaders about being part of Jesus' team, and what

it's like to be given a job by him. Allow the children to ask their own questions. Comment on how good it is to work with Jesus, and pray for the person who has been interviewed.

Finally remind the children about the Bench – a quiet place where they can sit and think, and maybe chat to one of the Ground Staff. Send the teams off to the next activities.

 CHANGE ENDS
(45 minutes)

Time out
Serve the refreshments – you could continue the theme of the Bible story by serving different kinds of bread. Chat together about today's story. What do they think of Jesus so far? After a short time go on to explore the Bible further:

- With older children
- With younger children
- With all age groups

Adapt these questions and discussion starters for use with your group:

- How do you think Jesus' team felt as they set off on their adventure?
- What might people have thought as they watched the fish and bread feed 5,000 people or more?
- How could Jesus make the small amount of bread and fish be enough for everyone?

Trophy room
Make a craft from the list on pages 24 to 26. If you have done the same craft over the first two days, you might want to change to a new project – one which the whole team works on together that would be appropriate for today's theme. When it's finished, display it in your team's dugout. Remember to use this time to chat as you all work together.

Stadium
Select games from the list on page 27 or do the personal best activities. Remember to record the children's new personal bests in their *Matchday*

Programmes. If you are doing three different activities, the children should achieve a personal best in at least one. Remember to be encouraging during the personal best activities!

 GRANDSTAND 2
(20 minutes)

Slam Dunk!
Welcome everyone back and sing a song. Read out any new jokes or questions and announce tomorrow's category ('What do you call a…?' jokes).

A question of sport (and other things!)
Cricket scored
As before, split the teams into two groups, combining different teams. Have a mix of questions as usual.

To score, write 0, 1, 2, 3, 4 and 6 on foam balls (have several of each number) and put them in a bag. After a correct answer, a child picks a ball from the bag. Their team score the number of runs on the ball. The group with the highest score wins!

'Wembley Way' part 2
Remind the children of what happened in the first half of today's drama. Will Curly tell Sam that he prayed for his leg?

Champion's Challenge
Sing the *Learn and remember* verse song again. Ask the children what they think Jesus meant when he said 'Forget about yourself'?

One presenter should hold up a mirror and look at themselves in it, checking their hair and turning this way and that to look at their image. The other presenter should explain that this is like thinking about yourself a lot. It's as if 'you' matter most – what you look like, what other people think when they see you. It's not wrong to look in mirrors to check that our hair looks tidy or that we haven't got Marmite smeared round our mouth! But if we want to follow

Jesus then we mustn't spend all our time thinking about me, me, me, me, me! To forget ourselves is to think about other people, and especially to think about Jesus.

If you're doing a different memory verse each day, learn Luke 9:23 today.

Prayer and songs
Tell the children that you are going to thank God for all the teammates at CHAMPION'S CHALLENGE. Say that when you say, 'Thank you for…' the children should shout out the names of two of their team, eg 'Thank you God for Clare and Adam!' Then say this prayer:

Dear God, thank you that we are all different, but that you have jobs for each of us to do. Thank you for all the teammates we have at CHAMPION'S CHALLENGE. Thank you God for … (Pause.) Amen.

End with the CHAMPION'S CHALLENGE song and then send teams back to their dugouts.

Team time (5 minutes)
When you are back in your dugout, talk about the day's highlights. You might want to practise your team shout, if you made one up, or recap the *Learn and remember* verse. Give out any craft, etc that needs to be taken home. Make sure you know how every child is going home.

 WARM DOWN

After the Ground Staff have tidied up, meet together to debrief. Use the feedback system that works best for you.

Have a short time of prayer where Team Captains and Vice-Captains pray for their groups, and other teams pray for their particular areas of responsibility.

Finish by doing any necessary preparation for the next session.

TEAM SHEET 3

TEAM MATE

LUKE 9:1–6, 10–17

Look at this picture of Jesus' squad giving out the food.

How many loaves and fish can you find?

Jesus fed over 5,000 people with five small loaves of bread and two fish! What name would you give Jesus after hearing that?

Write or draw what you think in this fish.

Then show or tell your team and team captain! Use the words that everyone has written in their fish to pray to Jesus. Tell him what you think of him!

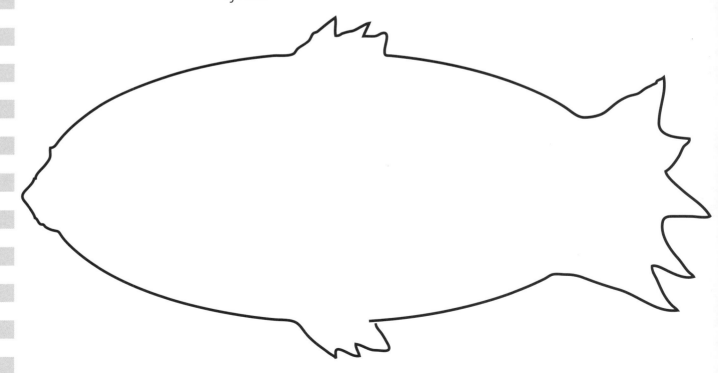

Psst! There are ten loaves and four fish hidden in the picture! But Jesus fed over 5,000 people with half that food!

DAY 4 SUBSTITUTE

PREMIER PASSAGE
Luke 22:47–53; 23

PREMIER THEME
Jesus takes the punishment in our place.

PREMIER AIMS
To understand that Jesus had done nothing wrong but was killed because the leaders were jealous of him. They didn't like him telling them they weren't doing things God's way. God used this to do something amazing…

TODAY'S THEME AND THE WORLD OF A CHILD
Most children hate the idea of being punished for something they did not do; 'It's not fair!' will be their cry. Jesus' death on the cross was not fair; little wonder that some adults cannot cope with the idea of substitution. You may find some of the more knowledgeable boys want to explain how substitution works in sport. It will doubtless build them up to do that, but try to stay focused on what Jesus did. You are telling them one of the most wonderful truths imaginable.

GROUND STAFF PREPARATION

SPIRITUAL PREPARATION

Read about it
Read Luke 23:13–25 together.

Think about it
'Substitution' is not an easy concept to understand. We have to avoid going in too deep with the children and confusing them, but need to grasp it for ourselves as it is such an amazing gift from God! In sport, substitution is about exchanging players because one is tired, or there is a need for a tactical change. A good substitution can swing a game. In the Bible (the word itself is not used in the Bible but the idea is present in several places) it is about Jesus being punished for our wrong (see Romans 5:6–8, 1 Peter 3:18). The analogy is not accurate. In sport a sub cannot come on when a player has been sent off for committing an offence. And yet that's exactly what Jesus did!

The Jewish Law stated clearly where God's boundaries lay (read the Ten Commandments in Deuteronomy 5 if you want a reminder) and it was obvious that everyone would have broken them in some way and so be separated from God, deserving his punishment for their wrongdoing. Barabbas, the murderer, was being punished under the law of the land for his crimes but was also separated from God because of his sins. On a human level, the Jewish authorities wanted Jesus dead and Pilate was too weak to stand up to them, and so he released Barabbas and had Jesus killed – a substitution in the sporting sense.

At the same time, on a spiritual level, God fulfilled his plans to deal once and for all with the issue of human sin, and bring people back to himself. So Jesus became a 'substitute' in the theological sense. God did a double switch: the blame – and therefore punishment – for all our sins went onto Jesus and his 'right' relationship with God became ours. We are given a picture of this through the interchange between Jesus and the criminals. To the one who recognises the innocence of Jesus and asks to be remembered when he ascends to the throne of his kingdom, Jesus gives the assurance that the substitution is made: 'Today you will be with me in paradise.'

As the Son of God, Jesus could have simply walked off the cross or called down legions of angels to rescue him. But he chose not to. To do so would have saved him pain and agony but would have left the rest of humanity far from God. In the passage today we celebrate with thankfulness all that God offers to us through this life-changing substitute.

Talk about it

- How does this passage challenge you?
- What do you want to say to Jesus as a result of reading this passage?

Pray about it

Spend a short time praying silently your answer to the above questions. Then together pray for the children, the Bible teaching and those who will explain the Scripture, for the activities and conversations that will happen today.

PRACTICAL PREPARATION

- As Ground Staff, spend time talking through the timetable.
- Set up team dugouts with everything needed for 'Team times'.
- Check that all other resources are ready in place.

Equipment checklist

- Registration desk – forms, team lists, pens, any information for parents, etc
- Team dugouts – ball and sweets; stickers; paper and pens for jokes; large sheet of paper and pens for questions; team lists, Bibles, copies of *Matchday Programme* or *Team*

Sheets

- Presenters – Slam Dunk basket, custard pies (eg flan cases filled with Dream Topping), moist face cloth, Bibles, pictures to illustrate the Bible narrative (see page 40), the word 'Substitute' written in large letters on a sheet of card, 2 team shirts or T-shirts with numbers on them (one of which is muddy), a quiz scoreboard, quiz questions, the running order
- Drama – costumes and props (see page 33)
- Technical team – any PA system, acetates and OHP/PowerPoint presentations, a laptop and projector
- Activities – equipment for games and craft
- Snack Bar – refreshments

PROGRAMME

Play some lively music and display the CHAMPION'S CHALLENGE logo to welcome the children as they arrive and are registered. Have a welcome team on hand to greet them and take them to their team dugout. If you know of any children of whom a close relative or friend has died recently you may want to warn their parent/carer (out of the child's hearing) that you are talking about Jesus' death today. Ask if it would be helpful to tell the child in advance, and keep the parent's wishes in mind as you work. Be prepared to give any grieving children time and space to talk – perhaps on the Bench.

TEAM TIME
(10 minutes)

What you need:

- A large soft ball
- Three sweets per person

Make any new children especially welcome and see what the children can remember from the first three days of the club. What has been their favourite story so far? Can anyone remember the *Learn and remember*

verse(s)? Any jokes or questions can be placed in the Slam Dunk basket. Then spend some time together on this activity.

Safe hands

Stand the team around the captain and give each child three sweets. Play a simple game of throwing and catching the ball round the circle and explain that they will lose a sweet if they don't catch it. When someone misses the ball, take a sweet away from someone else in the group – with younger ones, this will need to be a leader, but older ones will understand it better if sweets are taken from them.

Play this for a short time and then talk about it – how it feels to be punished for something you did not do. Ask if anyone would have been willing to give away sweets when someone else had dropped the ball.

 GRANDSTAND 1
(40 minutes)

Play the CHAMPION'S CHALLENGE song as everyone joins the larger group. The presenters should remind the children who they are and welcome any new children to the club. Remind everyone about the Slam Dunk basket.

Warm up

As in previous days, lead a workout to music with a strong beat. Put together a mix of movements that you have done so far, but be mindful of including children with special needs.

Songs

Sing the CHAMPION'S CHALLENGE song, together with one or two songs that you have already sung at the club – no doubt the children will have their favourites by now!

Champion team challenge

Explain that when the whistle blows, each team must get into a line and pass a ball down the line by twisting from one side to the other. When the ball reaches the back that person runs to the front and repeats this until everyone has had a turn. Teams must sit down when they have completed the challenge. Captains are not allowed to take part, but should encourage their teams. Before you begin, announce that instead of there being a prize for the winners there will be a forfeit for the losers: a custard pie in the face!

When the losers are discovered, line the whole team up at the front and then tell them that instead of everyone getting custard pies, just one will get it – the team captain! Do this quickly and then send them off to be cleaned up, but make no comment on it.

Wembley Way
Recap on the story of 'Wembley Way' so far. Who will own up to the grafitti?!

Today's training tip (TTT): Substitute
Pick up the theme from the drama with a mime of two people shaking hands and changing places as they do in a football or rugby match. If the children don't guess it quickly, say that today's title is 'Substitute' and whilst showing the word explain that this means a player who comes on to take the place of another. Comment on the shock of what happened in the drama. But that was nothing to what Jesus did…

Tell the story
Watch episode 4 of the CHAMPION'S CHALLENGE DVD or tell the Bible story as below:

Here's a coin. *(Hold up a familiar coin or show a picture of one.)* On this side it says how much it's worth. Is it the same on the other side? No. So at the start of a football or rugby match the referee tosses it up in the air like this *(Toss the coin.)* and one team calls for heads or… *(Encourage the children to shout 'tails'.)* That decides

who kicks off to start the match. Two sides of the same coin. Well, I'm going to tell you what happened next in Luke's book, but like this coin, it has two sides. Let's begin with… *(Toss the coin.)* tails!

(Use the pictures from page 40, the website or DVD-ROM section of the DVD to illustrate the story – either on PowerPoint, acetate or drawn on large sheets of paper – you can do this by projecting the picture onto paper with an OHP, drawing the outlines and then colouring them in. Be sure to have a Bible in your hand, opened at the passage, as you tell the story.)

This week we've heard about some of the wonderful things that Jesus did: making people like the soldier's servant better, feeding hungry people, welcoming lots of people onto his team as he told them how much God loved them. *(Show picture 1.)* Jesus, the Son of God, never did anything wrong. But some of the religious leaders didn't like him. He was more popular than them, and they were jealous of him. He told them very clearly that they weren't doing things God's way, and they didn't like that. So, although Jesus the Son of God never did anything wrong, they decided to get rid of him: to have him killed. *(Show picture 2.)* Late one night, when Jesus was praying in a garden and his friends were with him, some soldiers came and arrested him. And, although Jesus the Son of God never thought anything wrong, never said anything wrong and never did anything wrong, they took him away as a prisoner, to the governor of the city. *(Show picture 3.)*

The governor asked Jesus lots of questions and thought he should be set free. But the religious leaders didn't want this. Instead, they shouted for the governor to release Barabbas, a man who had killed someone. And the more the governor tried to set Jesus free, the more the leaders shouted for Barabbas. So in the end

the governor gave them what they wanted: he let the killer go free, and said that Jesus would be killed instead.

And so a few hours later, Jesus was nailed to a cross of wood. *(Show picture 4.)*

There was a sign over his head that said: 'The king of the Jews'. Two other men were killed on crosses alongside Jesus. They had both done things wrong. One of them shouted at Jesus: 'If you're God's Son, why don't you save yourself and us?' But the other one told him off: 'You and I are being punished for what we did wrong. But this man has done nothing wrong.' And then he said to Jesus, 'When you come as king, remember me.'

Jesus said to the man, 'Today, you'll be with me in paradise.' – that means the place where God's people are happy and at rest.

Later that day, Jesus shouted to God in a loud voice: 'Father, I put myself in your hands!' And then he died.

(Pause briefly.) That's one side of what happened. Now here's the other side, God's side: *(Turn the coin over in a big gesture.)* heads!

Do you remember what today's word is? *(Show the word.)* A substitute comes on to play if anyone is injured, or very tired later on in the game, or if they're not playing well. The coach hopes that by putting a substitute, the game can be turned round and they can win it.

There's one time when a substitute can't come on for another player, and that's when the player has been sent off for doing something wrong. Maybe they've kicked someone; maybe they've made a dangerous tackle. Whatever it is, it will have been against the rules and they get punished for it. And the team have to play on without them: the coach is not allowed then to put on a substitute. That's the rules in sport.

There are rules in life too, and God made them. He gave us really important rules like 'don't tell lies, don't kill people, don't steal, and be happy with what you've got.' But, sadly, we all break them at some time or other. And as we break the rules, we spoil our friendship with God. The Bible tells us that God loves us so much that he chose to mend the friendship. And this is how he did it. God swapped things round between us and Jesus. So when Jesus died on the cross, even though he had done nothing wrong, he took the punishment, instead of you and me, for all the wrong things that we – and everyone else in the whole world – have ever done and will ever do. All the lies or telling tales, all the cheating, all the fighting: all the wrong things that are ever done or thought or said. No matter how hard we try, we can't ever mend things between God and us. But Jesus could, because he is God's Son.

If we believe that Jesus is God's Son, and we ask him to forgive us for what we've got wrong, he does. Jesus becomes our substitute and we swap places. God looks at us, and sees us as if we are Jesus! We are forgiven, and our friendship with God is mended. It's like that first game you played in your teams, where someone else had their sweet taken away; it's like the team captain getting the custard pie instead of the team; it's like Curly clearing the litter and cleaning the wall while Jo played Miniball. It's like the criminal who died alongside Jesus – he knew Jesus was the king and he asked Jesus to remember him. And Jesus promised they would be together that very day in God's place of happiness. The criminal was forgiven. It's amazing!

You might think that's crazy! Or you might think, 'That's what I would like.' Well you can ask God to forgive you at any time: thank Jesus for being your substitute, and ask God to have you in his team. And he will. You can talk about that with your captain, or

during 'Time out', or you can come to the Bench any time and ask someone to explain it to you again.

And tomorrow we'll tell you the next incredible thing that happened in Luke's amazing stories of Jesus!

Song

Sing a suitable song, but even if this is a quiet song, have the children stand up as they will have been sitting for a while.

Prayer

Over their regular shirts, the presenters should put on the football/rugby shirts or T-shirts with numbers on the back, one of which should be very muddy. Show the difference between the shirts. Then exchange shirts and point out that the other person now has the muddy shirt – which is like Jesus taking on all our wrongs and us becoming like him.

Ask everyone to sit quietly for a minute and think about things that they do or think or say that are wrong. Then they must decide if they are really sorry for those things and want to ask Jesus to forgive them and help them to stop doing them. Play some quiet music for a minute or so while everyone thinks. Then pray out loud on behalf of everyone, saying sorry and asking Jesus to forgive these things. You might want to show the word 'sorry' as you do this.

Match of the day

Interview one of the leaders about how it feels to be forgiven because of Jesus' death. (Make sure the situation they will talk about is suitable for the children.) After a while, allow the children to ask their own questions.

Finally remind everyone of the Bench – somewhere to go and talk if they have questions or want someone to pray with them. Announce 'Change ends' and send the teams off to their various destinations.

CHANGE ENDS
(45 minutes)

If you are doing these activities in rotation, remember to change the order in which the teams do each one.

Time out

Serve the refreshments and chat together about the club so far. Then go on to explore today's Bible story further:

- With older children
- With younger children
- With all age groups

Adapt these questions and discussion starters for use with your group:

- What sort of things that hurt God do people that you know do?
- How can you and I be forgiven?
- How does that make you feel?
- Talk about how amazing it is to be forgiven. How do people feel when that happens? Some are so thrilled when they realise it that they want to become one of Jesus' followers – to join his team! Explain what it means to follow Jesus – believing he is God's Son, saying sorry for the wrong things you do, and asking him to help you live by God's way day by day.

You might want to use one of the following booklets to help you: *Friends with Jesus* (for 5 to 7s), *Me+Jesus* (for 8s and 9s) and *Jesus=Friendship Forever* (for 10 to 12s). All are published by Scripture Union (see the inside front cover).

Trophy room

Make a craft from the selection on pages 24 to 26. You should, by now, have a good idea about which teams like doing which craft, so you could take that into consideration when choosing the craft.

Stadium

Select games from the list given on pages 26 and 27. If you are only doing 'Personal best' work on three days during the club, miss it out today.

 ### GRANDSTAND 2
(20 minutes)

Slam Dunk!

Welcome everyone back and sing a song. Read out any new jokes, comments and questions, and ask for everyone's best jokes for tomorrow.

A question of sport (and other things!)
Rounders scored

Create two rounders pitches on card, acetate or in PowerPoint. Ask questions alternately to the two teams and move them on one post round their pitch for a correct answer. The highest number of rounders wins! Remember to change the combination of teams competing together for today's quiz.

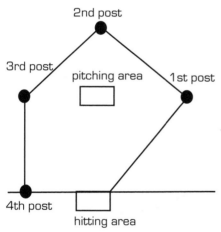

Champion's Challenge

Recap the Learn and remember verse. Either sing the song, or write one or two words of the verse on slips of paper and stick them to different sporting gloves (see page 59 for how to split up the verse). Use the gloves of a goalkeeper, wicketkeeper, baseball player, golfer, hockey keeper – whatever you can gather together. Hide the gloves around the room and ask the children to find them.

Whoever finds a glove should bring it to the front and put it on. Ask everyone to put the verse in the right order and then read it together a couple of times.

Explain that when Jesus 'took up his cross' he was being obedient to God. He didn't do it because God was cruel and bossy, but because God loved everyone in the world, and wanted to mend their friendship, as we heard earlier. So when it says 'take up your cross each day' it doesn't mean we are going to be killed, it means that people who follow Jesus show their love for him by obeying him.

If you are having a different memory verse each day Romans 5:8 speaks about Jesus being a substitute for us.

Prayer and songs

Pray, thanking Jesus for being a substitute for us. End with the CHAMPION'S CHALLENGE song and then send the teams back to their dugouts.

 ### TEAM TIME
(5 minutes)

Play the ball game that you played at the beginning of the session again. This time, give everyone a sticker when they catch or drop the ball. Chat about the day's events and be ready to pray with any children who would like it. Don't make a big thing out of this, or make it last a long time. But make sure each child has a copy of the appropriate commitment booklet (see inside front cover), if you are using them.

 ### WARM DOWN

After the Ground Staff have cleared up meet to debrief. Ask for any comments, using the feedback system that most suits you, to identify anything that needs reworking for tomorrow.

Staying all together, end with a prayer time, praying especially for the children who have shown a particular interest in today's teaching. Go on to mention every child in the club by name.

Finish by doing any necessary preparation for tomorrow.

SUBSTITUTE

LUKE 22:47–53; 23

Some people didn't like Jesus. They tried to stop him saying all the things he was saying. In the end, one of Jesus' squad betrayed him!

Read Luke 22:47–53.

Complete the faces below for each of the verses to show how Jesus' squad must have been feeling.

Verse 47

Verse 50

Verse 51

When he died on the cross, Jesus took all the punishment that was meant for us, because of all the things we have done wrong. Make a list of all the people who did the wrong thing in this story.

Talk about it together.

Jesus died for them. He died for us too.

Because he died, we can be friends with God!

> Thank you Jesus that you died and took the punishment instead of us.

Use the codebreaker to find out what happened next!

⚽ = a ⚾ = e 🎾 = i 🏉 = u

J🎾s⚽s c⚽m⚾ ⚽l🎾v⚾ ⚽g⚾🎾n!

J_s_s c_m_ _l_v_ _g__n!

DAY 5 WINNER

PREMIER PASSAGE
Luke 24:1–35

PREMIER THEME
Jesus is alive! Jesus defeats death and is alive for ever! He appears to his followers and explains the good news.

PREMIER AIMS
To ensure the children know that Jesus came alive again, and is alive today!

TODAY'S THEME AND THE WORLD OF A CHILD
This narrative will be of no surprise to children who have grown up in church, but to any who have no church background it may be hard to grasp. It is one thing to cope with him doing miracles, but another to accept that he came alive again. Some will be unsurprised, having read or seen *The Lion, The Witch and The Wardrobe*, but the important thing for them is to recognise that Luke's Gospel is not a work of fiction but is truth. And this may be the first time they have heard it!

GROUND STAFF PREPARATION

SPIRITUAL PREPARATION

Read about it
Read Luke 24:1–11 together.

Think about it
This really is an amazing story! We can never fully understand how it must have felt for the women and then the other disciples. Think of a play, book or film where the ending has been totally different from what you expected (don't tell each other or it might spoil it for someone else!) and remember your amazement, surprise and shock at the difference.

The women's grief must have been great, that they went to Jesus' tomb at the first opportunity; they may also have been terrified of the consequences of being known as his followers. This mix of emotions must have been compounded by the disappearance of Jesus' body – here was even more unfinished business. And then the appearance of the angels must have almost frightened them to death! Yet, in the midst of all this, they remembered what Jesus had said. And so they had faith, despite the reception they got from the disciples! I wonder what they thought that evening when Jesus had appeared to Peter, Cleopas and the other disciple. There might have been a temptation to say, 'We told you so!' When something amazing happens like this it is important that we don't get caught up in making our name known for having believed/seen/remembered, but that we celebrate the glory that rightly goes to the name of Jesus!

Talk about it
• What has Jesus said that you need to remember today?
• What do you want to say to the risen Lord?

Pray about it

Spend time praising God for his work in bringing Jesus alive again. Pray for the children, that they will grasp this too, and for all that God will do today. Ask God to give you eyes to see how he is at work.

PRACTICAL PREPARATION

Today's Bible narrative includes an interview with Cleopas, one of the disciples who walked with Jesus to Emmaus. There are three ways you can do this:

- Simple – create a TV screen out of an appropriately painted cardboard box with holes cut in it either back and front or front and bottom. Either stand it on a table and sit Cleopas behind it (front and rear holes) or sit him on a chair with the box over his head (front and bottom holes!)
- Safe – If you have access to a camcorder, record an interview between Cleopas and one of the presenters. Then show this as if it's a news clip.
- Snazzy – Record Cleopas's side of the interview only – allow time for introductions by the presenter, for each question to be asked and then Cleopas speaks his answers. Allow time for the presenter to thank Cleopas before ending the interview. Have Cleopas wear an earpiece to add to the effect as if on a live-link with the studio! This will need careful rehearsal by the presenter if it is to be convincing by getting the timing right!

NB This can be great fun to do – the 'snazzy' version is especially effective – but do not let it take over from the even more fantastic story that it tells!

Today focuses on Jesus' resurrection, but in order to make the point of how amazing that is, the children need to understand the finality of death. Even if they have experienced the death of a friend or relative they may not have grasped that it is for ever. Be sensitive in the way that you deal with this and be ready to help children

who are upset. As you explain this through the story, do not digress onto Christian teaching about eternal life; despite its importance, to do so will only confuse the children. Save that for another occasion!

- As Ground Staff, spend time talking through the timetable.
- Set up team dugouts with everything needed for medals.
- Check that all other resources are ready in place.

Equipment checklist

- Registration desk – forms, team lists, pens, any information for parents
- Team dugouts – equipment for medals; paper and pens for jokes; paper and pen for Champion's Challenge; large sheets of paper and pens for questions; team lists, Bibles, copies of *Matchday Programme* or *Team Sheets*
- Presenters – Slam Dunk basket, questions for game, Bibles, script if needed for Cleopas interview; flowers, bottle of perfume, stone, strips of cloth, two white T-shirts, map and script for talk; quiz scoreboard, quiz questions, supporter's scarf or other item, the running order
- Cleopas – costume and TV, if using this method
- Drama – costumes and props (see page 34)
- Technical team – any PA system, acetates and OHP/PowerPoint presentations, a laptop and projector
- Activities – equipment for games and craft
- Snack Bar – refreshments

PROGRAMME

Play some lively music and display the CHAMPION'S CHALLENGE logo to welcome the children as they arrive and are registered. Have a welcome team on hand to greet them and take them to their team dugout. Be as celebratory as you can, as this is the

last day of CHAMPION'S CHALLENGE and today's Bible story is a cause for huge celebration!

 **TEAM TIME**
(10 minutes)

What you need:

- either foil-covered cardboard circles and blunt pencils
- or circles of card with a medal design on (see page 42) and felt-tip pens
- hole punch
- ribbon

Welcome all the children to CHAMPION'S CHALLENGE and use this time at the start of the club to gauge the children's reactions to yesterday's story. Ask if anyone can remember the *Learn and remember* verse(s). Make sure you tell the team that today's story about Jesus is an amazing one! Remind children about the Slam Dunk basket and then spend time together doing this activity.

Medal making

If you are using the foil-covered card medals, then show the children how to gently etch a medal design onto the foil medal with a blunt pencil, taking care not to scratch through the foil. When they have finished, punch a hole in the top and thread a length of ribbon through the hole.

If you are using the card medals, give out the medals and felt-tip pens and encourage the children to personalise their medal. Again, punch a hole at the top and thread a length of ribbon through.

Whilst doing this, chat with the children about what they have enjoyed through the week.

 **GRANDSTAND 1**
(40 minutes)

Play the CHAMPION'S CHALLENGE song as everyone joins the larger group. The presenters should remind the children who they are and welcome any new children to the club.

Remind everyone that this is the last chance to have a joke read out from the Slam Dunk basket!

Warm up

Lead an energetic warm up to music with a strong beat. Put together a routine using the most popular movements from this week. Keep the energy up and make sure all the Ground Staff join in!

Songs

Sing the CHAMPION'S CHALLENGE song, together with one of the children's favourite songs.

Champion team challenge

Explain that the teams have one minute to tell their team captain all the things about Jesus that they have heard this week. Try and get feedback from each team and congratulate everyone on remembering so much!

Wembley Way

Remind the children what happened yesterday and then watch today's episode.

Today's training tip (TTT): Winner

Enact a short mime of 'winner' – one presenter should run in slow motion past the other to win a race. Ask the children what they think today's title is. Show the word. In Day 4, it seemed like Jesus was the loser, but today something special happens…

Tell the story

Remind the children where the story ended yesterday. Then watch episode 5 of the CHAMPION'S CHALLENGE DVD or tell the Bible story as provided below.

When do you say goodbye? *(Ask for suggestions.)* Saying goodbye is something that we do lots of times each day – you might shout it as you run out to play, or as you wave to your mum, your dad, your baby sister or your pet rabbit on your way to school in the morning. Sometimes it's just a way of being polite and making sure that the other person knows you are leaving, but with friends and family it sort of means, 'I'm going, but I'm looking forward to seeing you again.'

When someone dies, their friends and family have a special time – often in a church – to say 'goodbye' to them. It's called a funeral. It's a very important time, because when someone dies they really have gone forever. So saying this last 'goodbye' means lots of things like 'thank you for being special', 'I will miss you' and 'I love you'. Sometimes people take flowers too. *(Show a bunch of flowers.)*

Very early on the Sunday morning after Jesus died some of his friends went to say their last 'goodbye' to him. You see, when Jesus died on the Friday it was almost the start of the special day in the week when everybody rested and nobody went anywhere. Jesus' dead body had been quickly put in a rocky hole, a tomb, and a huge stone had been pushed in front of it. His friends had no chance to say 'goodbye', to cry and be sad, to think about all the great times they had had with him. They just had to go home quickly, and wait until the special day was over.

So very early on Sunday morning some of the women who were his friends went to say 'goodbye'. They took with them some lovely smelling perfumes to put with his body, *(Show the perfume bottle.)* forgetting that there was a huge stone in front of the tomb. *(Show the stone.)*

But when they got to the tomb, something was wrong! The stone wasn't in front of the tomb! They went in, and found something else that wasn't as they expected: Jesus' dead body had gone! *(Show the strips of cloth.)* Suddenly there were two men in shining clothes *(Show the two white T-shirts.)* standing beside them: were they angels? Jesus' friends were terrified!

'Why are you looking in the place where you find dead people for someone who is alive?' the men asked. 'Jesus isn't here: he's alive! Don't you remember what he told you a long time ago: that he would be killed on a cross and come alive again?'

Then the women did remember, and they went to tell the rest of Jesus' squad. They could hardly believe their ears!

Later in the day, two friends were walking home from Jerusalem to a town about seven miles away – about as far as from here to *[name somewhere about seven miles from you that the children will know]. (Show the map.)* Here is Cleopas, one of the two friends!

Pres: Cleopas, tell us how it all began!

Cleo: Well the two of us were walking back home from Jerusalem, talking about everything that had happened, when this man came and walked along with us.

Pres: Did you know who he was?

Cleo: No, we didn't have a clue – it was getting dark, and we were thinking a lot, you know?

Pres: So what happened?

Cleo: This man asked us what we were talking about. He could see that we were sad, but we couldn't believe his question: I mean who could have been in Jerusalem and NOT know what had been happening?! So we told him, 'Our friend Jesus, who came from God and did wonderful things, has been killed. Some women who were his friends too, have told us he's alive again, but nobody has seen him.'

Pres: What did the man say next?

Cleo: He said, 'Long, long ago the prophets told people about God's special person who would come. They didn't know his name, but they knew he would come one day.'

Pres: Sorry – the profits? Are you

talking about money?

Cleo: No – you spell this one differently! The prophets were the people who talked about what God was doing and what God was going to do, and what God was saying. Anyway, starting with Moses and the prophets, this man explained how God's special person would have to suffer a lot and then be killed. Well, that was like Jesus, wasn't it? This man was making a lot of sense! Anyway we got back to Emmaus, and arrived at our house.

Pres: And the man left you then?

Cleo: He was going to, only it was late, and we'd enjoyed talking with him, so we asked him to come in.

Pres: Did he?

Cleo: He did. We got a quick meal ready and he took the bread, said thanks to God for it, and began to share it out. And then it happened! As he broke the bread, I remembered another time… some fish, some bread… five thousand people… plenty to eat… Well I think we both worked it out at the same time – this man was Jesus!

Pres: Jesus?!!

Cleo: Yeah, Jesus, right there in our house – alive! And then just as suddenly as we knew it was him, he'd gone! I don't know how and I don't know where, but we didn't stop to find out! We were so excited that we put on our coats again and went all the way back to Jerusalem to tell the rest of Jesus' team there. Another seven-mile walk – except that we ran when we could, we were so excited! You know, I'd thought there was something special about this man; when he talked to us I had this sort of warm glow creeping all through me. No wonder, is it? – it was Jesus!

Pres: And what did your friends say when you got back to Jerusalem?

Cleo: Well there's the funny thing – we went in all excited shouting

that they'd never guess what had happened, and someone said, 'You'll never guess what's happened – Jesus really IS alive and he's been to see Peter!' So it was party time all round!

Pres: A truly amazing story! Cleopas, thank you!

Cleo: You're welcome!

Round off the story by saying how amazing it all is!

Song

Sing a celebratory song, maybe one with lots of actions, so the children can join in with the amazing feeling of the story!

Match of the day

Interview one of the leaders about why it matters to them that Jesus is alive today. This is an important aspect of today's story and answers the question, 'Jesus is alive, what does that mean for me today?' Let the children ask a couple of questions if there is time.

Finally, remind the children about the Bench and then announce 'Change ends'. Send the teams off to their various areas.

 CHANGE ENDS
(45 minutes)

Time out

Serve your refreshments and chat together about all the stories you have heard this week as you eat and drink. Then go on to explore the Bible together:

• With older children
• With younger children
• With all ages groups

Adapt these questions and discussion starters for use with your group:

• How could Jesus come alive again? Who made it happen?
• If you had been walking along with Cleopas, what would you have asked Jesus?
• What do you think about Jesus

being alive again?
• You could discuss some of the questions that the children will undoubtably have. Try to talk about all their questions – one that you might think isn't important, could be significant to the child who is asking it.

Trophy room

Make a craft from the selection on pages 24 to 26. If you have started a craft activity earlier in the week which needs completing, this would be a good time to finish things off.

Stadium

Select games from the list on page 27. If you have been doing 'Personal best' work, then do a final session on it today. Make sure you record any new personal best in the child's *Matchday Programme*, if you're using it. Make a record of all the new personal bests the children have achieved, so that certificates can be made to be presented in Grandstand 2.

 GRANDSTAND 2
(20 minutes)

Slam Dunk!

Welcome everyone back and sing a song. Go through the jokes and questions in the Slam Dunk basket and thank everyone who has contributed throughout the club for doing so.

A question of sport (and other things!)
Basketball scored

Have two sets of questions: easy, scoring 1 point each; and hard, scoring three points. Teams can choose which type of question they would like to answer each time. If they fail to answer a 3 point question correctly they can have another try at a 1 point. The higher scoring team wins. Write each score down on an acetate/flipchart.

Champion's challenge

Sing the *Learn and remember* verse

song, if you have been using it, or ask for volunteers to recite the verse.

Show a football supporter's scarf or other item of team support and ask who supports that particular team. Explain that a true supporter will support their team whether they are at the top of the Premiership or the bottom of the lowest league! They are a supporter whether their team is winning or losing.

Sometimes, it's easy to follow Jesus – it feels good like your team winning the league! But sometimes, maybe if people tease you for being a Christian, it can be tough – and it feels like it does when your team loses week after week after week, and it's hard to be their supporter. But Jesus doesn't change, and if we're going to follow him then we must do so when it feels tough as well as when it feels great!

This is the real champion's challenge: to follow Jesus like this!

If you are having a different memory verse each day, Philippians 3:14 is an encouragement to keep running the race.

Prayer and songs
Do this prayer shout together:

Presenter: Jesus died and took our place!
Children: J-E-S-U-S!
Presenter: Jesus is alive today!
Children: J-E-S-U-S!
Presenter: Jesus is with us every day!
Children: J-E-S-U-S!
Presenter: Jesus is alive today!
Children: J-E-S-U-S!

Present the Personal Best certificates if you are using them. Then sing the CHAMPION'S CHALLENGE song and send teams back to their dugouts.

 TEAM TIME
(5 minutes)

Sit round in a circle and ask each player to think, 'What would you say to Jesus if he were sitting next to you now?' Give them time to think and then ask for some ideas.

Explain that although we can't see Jesus with our eyes or reach out and touch him with our hands, he is here! He's not a ghost, but he is alive and with us now. And Jesus hears us when we talk to him.

Ask all the players to sit quietly and tell Jesus in their heads what they want to say to him. End the time of quiet with an 'Amen' and then chat together until parents come to collect their children. Remember to give out everything they have made to take home, if they have not already done so. If you are having a special Sunday service to follow up the club, give out invitations now. If not, then make sure the children (and parents) know about your regular programme of children's and family work.

 WARM DOWN

If you are using a school, or another venue which isn't your church building, then you may have to have a longer clear-up time today. Remember to still have a debrief time. Ask for some stories of what God has done in children's (and Ground Staff's) lives during the week.

End with a short prayer time, thanking God for all that he has done. Pray too, for the children, that you will be able to keep contact and carry on encouraging them.

Do any necessary preparation for Sunday's service.

TEAM SHEET 5

WINNER

LUKE 24:1–35

Can you spot the ten differences between these two pictures?

When the women got to the tomb, Jesus wasn't there – he had come alive again! Read the story in Luke 24:1–12.

Jesus met two of his friends when they were on their way to a place called Emmaus. At first they did not know who he was! But then they recognised him and rushed off to tell their friends. You can read that story in Luke 24:13–35!

If you met Jesus, what would you say to him? Write or draw it here.

SUNDAY SERVICE 2

CHAMPION

PREMIER PASSAGE
Acts 1:1–8

PREMIER THEME
Jesus promises his Holy Spirit as the disciples' helper.

PREMIER AIMS
To show that the Holy Spirit came as Jesus promised, and to explain how he is at work today.

This could also be run as a club session for families. Use as much or as little of the outline to suit your situation, but be sure to include the Bible teaching and, if possible, the drama.

TODAY'S THEME AND THE WORLD OF A CHILD
Many children have invisible friends when they are young, but they are imaginary. They need to know that the Holy Spirit is equally invisible - but very real! Questions for some children – especially those who can only cope with concrete ideas - will include, 'How does he get inside you?' A good answer to these questions will enable you to move on to important things such as what he does and how he helps us.

WHAT YOU NEED
- A small gift for every child who has attended the club (a certificate, medal or bookmark)
- A kite

INTRODUCTION

The presenters should welcome everyone to this last session of CHAMPION'S CHALLENGE. If appropriate, read a few of the best jokes from the Slam Dunk basket.

Songs
Sing the CHAMPION'S CHALLENGE song. Between different sections of the service, include other songs that have gone particularly well.

Wembley Way
Give a short enough recap of what has happened during the week to make sense to anyone who has not seen each episode. Explain where Friday's drama ended, and introduce the final episode of 'Wembley Way'. At the end, comment on what has happened.

Champion's challenge
Recap Luke 9:23 and briefly explain the meaning of it as before for those who have not been at the club. Remind the children that the real champion's challenge is to follow Jesus like this. Then get everyone to say the verses again, or sing the *Learn and remember* verse song.

Bible reading
Introduce the reading with an explanation that this is the first part of Dr Luke's second book! Read Acts 1:1–8, using different people to speak the words of Jesus and the disciples.

Team talk
Show the certificates, medals or bookmarks (wait to give them out later, so that children will not be distracted by them through the talk). Comment that these are 'end of CHAMPION'S CHALLENGE' gifts: they are not leaving gifts, as you hope they will come again! But it is something to remind them of the week – of the things they have achieved, played, sung, made and discovered. Medals and certificates remind us of what we

have already achieved, and inspire us about what more we can achieve in the future.

When Jesus was going back to heaven he promised a gift to each of his team. This gift was the Holy Spirit, who would be with them and help them by making them powerful and brave to go on following Jesus. Just as your certificates/medals/bookmarks remind you of everything you've discovered this week, so the Holy Spirit would remind Jesus' team of all that Jesus had told them and all that Jesus had done. And the Holy Spirit would help them to do things that were just as amazing as the things Jesus did. What a great gift!

We can't see the Holy Spirit with our eyes, nor can we reach out and touch him with our hands, but he is here. We can't see him, but we can see what he does. Here's a picture of what I mean.

We can't see the wind, but we can see what it does! You may think this kite [Show the kite.] looks good here in church, but take it outside and watch what happens when the wind is blowing! The kite can do so much more then! When the wind is blowing through it, it's all that it was made to be.

So it is with everyone who follows Jesus: they can do so much more when the Holy Spirit is at work in them, and they can become all that they were made to be!

The people that Jesus had chosen to be in his team discovered that very quickly – you can read more about it in the book of Acts. Instead of being afraid and hiding away, they couldn't stop talking about Jesus to everyone they met. When Jesus first chose the fishermen to be in his team he told them that he would teach them to catch people instead of fish, and that's just what happened. They talked about Jesus everywhere, and the people began to follow Jesus. It was so exciting! And that all happened because the Holy Spirit helped them to be what Jesus chose them to be.

I wonder what the Holy Spirit can help you to do and to be. If you choose or have chosen to follow Jesus then he does the same for you. Jesus might not have chosen you to catch people for him; he might have chosen you to be a teacher or a bus driver, a secretary or a computer programmer, a parent or a pupil. Whatever it is, the Holy Spirit can help you to do that, to the best of your ability. Most of all, he will help you to be more and more like Jesus as you follow him.

Let's ask him to do that in a prayer. If you think 'that's what I want too,' then say 'Amen' at the end. Here's the prayer:

'Lord Jesus, thank you for your special gift, the Holy Spirit, who helps us to follow you and be like you.

Holy Spirit, please come and help me to be more and more like Jesus, and to be all that Jesus has chosen me to be.

Father God, thank you for this time at CHAMPION'S CHALLENGE. Please help me to know that you are with me day by day: now, at home, at school, at work, at play. Amen.'

Songs
Give out the gifts and then sing a cheerful 'Jesus' song or the CHAMPION'S CHALLENGE song

Blessing
End with a prayer of blessing.

Serve refreshments afterwards and encourage the Ground Staff to chat with the children and their families, perhaps asking what they have enjoyed the most, or asking parents and carers what they perceive their children have enjoyed most. Make sure that children take home any remaining craft. You could also run another craft activity after the service or session!

Be sure to have a couple of Ground Staff at the door to say goodbye as people leave.

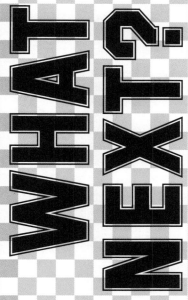

CHAMPION'S CHALLENGE TRAINING FEATURE

See the training feature, on following up your holiday club, for ideas and advice on expanding your ministry beyond the summer.

KEEPING IT GOING THROUGH THE YEAR!

The final whistle has blown on CHAMPION'S CHALLENGE, the last child has gone home and the Ground Staff are recuperating with a cup of tea after clearing away all the equipment. 'Well, only 51 weeks to the next!' says someone brightly.

Fifty-one weeks?! You might well groan that it will come round so quickly, but the children will doubtless groan that it is so far away. And they are right: they have had enormous fun, have loved making friends with other children and with the Ground Staff, and have enjoyed hearing the amazing stories and truths about Jesus. These are all good reasons to do more with the children and to do it much sooner than in a year's time, but the most important reason is this: if the good news of Jesus is worth telling then it should be told in this sort of manner far more than just once a year!

Here are six ways to help you build on your holiday club at different times of the year, enabling you to keep up contact with the children and keep on telling them about Jesus.

- Family sports activities. Check out the relevant section of this book for ideas.
- Regular family events. Devise a programme of different events, perhaps starting with a holiday club reunion, and then inviting families to a range of events that the church organises, such as a Harvest supper, Christmas party and so on right through the year. See *Celebrations Sorted* (Scripture Union) for ideas.

£5 OFF!

BUY £60 WORTH OF EXTRA CHAMPION'S CHALLENGE RESOURCES AND GET £5 OFF!

1. Take this to your local Christian Bookshop.
2. Send it to Scripture Union Mail Order, PO Box 5148, Milton Keynes MLO, MK2 2YX with your order and payment.
3. Visit our online shop at www.scriptureunion.org.uk and place your order online where the £5 discount will be applied.

CHAMPION'S CHALLENGE!

- Seasonal specials for children. What about a Christmas craft day or an Easter journey; a pancake party or Light party?
- Inset days. Run a club session when your local school's staff have a training day.
- Monthly or bi-monthly Saturday events. These might be morning club-style sessions or evening 'spectaculars'.
- Weekly club. Children rarely come to church on a Sunday unless their parents come too. If your church sees Sunday as the day for in-depth Bible teaching for children then a midweek club would be a better option for unchurched children. A weekly club should run along the same lines as holiday club, so that it has similar fun elements, as well as simple Bible teaching. It will help children to keep on meeting and getting to know Jesus. It can be very effective even if run for just half of each school term. You might run a lunchtime or after-school club in the school building, or an early evening club at church or in a community hall. See *Top Tips: Reaching Unchurched Children* for help on running a midweek club, or Scripture Union's SUPA Clubs web pages www.scriptureunion.org.uk/supaclubs for materials specifically for school clubs. Scripture Union publishes a number of programmes for midweek clubs in the eye level range, including *Target Challenge* which follows on from CHAMPION'S CHALLENGE. These offer a great opportunity for children to go on interacting with Christians and to see what they have heard at CHAMPION'S CHALLENGE worked out in the lives of the Ground Staff.

This voucher cannot be exchanged for cash or any other merchandise and cannot be used with any other offer. This offer includes the CHAMPION'S CHALLENGE resource book, DVD and *Matchday Programme* (singles and packs.) It does not include CPO publicity merchandise. Only single orders of £60 and above qualify for this offer.

TO THE RETAILER: Please accept this voucher as a discount payment.
CREDIT DUE: £5.00 less normal trade discount.
This voucher must be returned to:
STL Customer Services, PO Box 300,
Carlisle, Cumbria, CA3 0QS by 3rd September 2008.

NAME OF SHOP:_____

STL ACCOUNT NUMBER: _____

VOWCC08